# A Lasting Legacy

## Scrapbooks and Photo Albums that Touch the Heart

Souzzann Y.H. Carroll

Living Vision Press
Bountiful, Utah

ISBN 0-9663318-0-X

Living Vision Press
P.O. Box 326
Bountiful, UT 84011

cover and author photos by Al Thelin

# Acknowledgements

My appreciation and thanks go to all the wonderful family historians who have shared their knowledge, support, and enthusiasm with me over the last seven years. Though I risk leaving someone out, I want to mention some people who made important contributions to this work. I take complete responsibility for the final product, while acknowledging I could not have completed this book without the help of many generous individuals. If there are any mistakes, they are completely my own. Steven Puglia, Dale Heaps, Al Thelin, Jeanne English, and Borge Andersen were incredibly patient and helpful as I sifted through mountains of photo preservation and archival science publications. Jennia Hart, Vicky Sedgwick, Myndee Reed, Karen Oxford, Anna Swinney, Debbie Janasak, Kathryn Schein, Sara Anderson, Kindra Stein, Dynail Miller, Lori Ness, and Nadine Serrano were particularly helpful with my on-line research and recommendations for using the Internet as a scrapbooking resource. Rachel, Lori, Sian, Monique, Amy, Nancy D., Yuko, Kris, Nancy W. , Susie C. , Michelle, Missy, Janet M., Jerrene, Paula S., Lara S., Toni H., Debbie H., Cindy B., Jenny D., Bert R., Sarah S., and the on-line folks I know only as frog, Purrmaid, and Agnostic also have shared ideas, tips, and feedback that were very important in the completion of this book. I appreciate their willingness to share their ideas, humor, and information.

Kim Cook, Sherri Henrie, Aneisa Phelps, Jeanne Reed, and especially Tracey Isidro contributed expertise, moral support, and most importantly their shining examples of the scrapbooking community at its best. Without them, this book would still be just a pile of my personal notes. Kris, Ali, Brendan, Colleen, Michelle, and Doug gave of their talents when I needed them the most. A special thanks to Robert Dilts, who taught me to balance dreaming and putting the dream into action.

Special appreciation goes to Gabrell and Logan, who were always there for me when I needed them the most. My editors, Jen Alves and Jared Fields, were unfailingly diligent, patient, and supportive through the final push to create this book. I could not have done it without them.

For
Marion Hughes McEntire, Sara Lee Hughes Lake
and especially for my mother, Laura Hughes Hockery

# Contents

# Preface

Creating memory albums, or scrapbooks, is one of the most rewarding activities we do. These records of our families, our experiences, and our deepest joys are timeless gifts we give ourselves. Our albums frequently become the most treasured possessions of our family members. All over the world, people are discovering the satisfaction which comes from telling the stories of their families, their friends, and their own lives.

Thousands of people are discovering the joys of scrapbooking. Consider the following numbers. *Creating Keepsakes* magazine premiered in the fall of 1996. It has since become the most popular place to advertise for companies selling memory album supplies. According to *Creating Keepsakes*, a Rose Market Research reader survey indicates that their May/June 1998 issue will be read by over 480,000 scrapbook enthusiasts.

Over 30,000 independent consultants sell the products of the Creative Memories direct sales company. The only items offered are scrapbook albums and supplies used to create the finished pages. They are the originators of a marathon scrapbooking event reminiscent of old-fashioned quilting bees. "Crop 'til you drop" is a trademark of Creative Memories that refers to a gathering of people who work for hours, sometimes all night, on their scrapbooks. They share ideas, snacks, moral support, and supplies. Usually, many of the tools they use are owned by the consultant who charges a fee and holds the event in her home. Most of these consultants, almost all women, live in the United States. However, Creative Memories also has branched out to Canada, the United Kingdom, Australia, and Mexico.

In 1996 and 1997, over one hundred scrapbook supply stores opened and other types of stores shifted their inventory to include several aisles of scrapbook products. One Internet site devoted to scrapbooking lists over 500 stores in its directory of retail sources of supplies. Entrepreneurs have recognized that part of the appeal of scrapbooking is participation with other interested people. They offer classes on scrapbooking, but also sponsor workshops that give customers a place to work, provide tools such as cutters, templates, and usually the expertise of a scrapbooking teacher.

Almost 30 years ago, I compiled my first scrapbooks and photo albums. The type of album I describe in this book, however, is relatively new. My older albums had photos in some books and paper memorabilia in others. I included very little written information; just a caption or name here and there. My vision of what makes a memory album changed in 1981. I was fortunate enough to spend an hour or so at an exhibit that featured the memory albums of the Christensen family. Marielen Christensen compiled 50 volumes of books detailing the history of her family, including several ancestors. Her collection consisted primarily of album after album of photographs, paper memorabilia, letters, and extensive narratives of her family's experiences. This exhibit inspired my desire to put together an album that combined the photographs, newspaper clippings, postcards, and other keepsakes that told the story of my deceased father and particularly of his experiences as a fighter pilot in World War II and the Korean War.

In the late 1980s, I met Jeanne English, owner of Restoration Source, and discovered the Creative Memories products. Through reading Jeanne's book, *Preserving the Precious*®, conversations with her, and other research, I found that the great majority of the supplies sold to create scrapbooks and photo albums were actually quite harmful to photographs. I looked at the self-stick albums and black paper scrapbooks I had assembled around 1970 and was determined to create something better. Since I had decided to do a lot of documentation and decorate my album pages to enhance the photographs, I wanted the finished books to last as long as possible. Since my sons never met my father, I wanted these albums to be a way for them to know him a little. Looking forward, I also wanted to create memory books that, from their pages, would allow future generations to know me and my family.

From my own experience and my observations of those around me, I know it is useful to look inside and seek to heal any part of the self that is hurt. Learning and striving for self-improvement are valuable activities. In the time of self-help books and talk show therapy, however, sometimes we focus too much on what is wrong with our lives. Scrapbooks are important, in part, because they celebrate who we are. Assembling them causes us to pay attention to the successes, the joys, and the victories of life. The aspects of our experience on which we focus tend to grow. By guiding us to notice and dwell on the beauty and goodness we see, scrapbooks move us toward more of those experiences.

This book is primarily the result of gathering information about scrapbooking for my own use. As I shared my findings and ideas through classes, on-line discussions, and sessions with other scrapbookers, this book took shape. Rather than copying any of my layouts, or anyone elses, I hope you will use this book to develop your own style. I would like the ideas in this book to be a jumping off point, or springboard, to creating scrapbooks in your own way. Write notes in it and add your own tips and techniques. It is designed to be a workbook that you personalize. My goal is to assist people in creating memory albums that are personally meaningful, attractive, and very durable. If readers have fun, exercise their creativity, and make this process a joyful part of their lives, the project is a success.

# PART I

# Reasons and Rewards

# *Introduction*

You have some interest in preserving and showcasing your photos and memorabilia, or you would not be reading this book. Consider for a moment your goals for your scrapbooks. This book will be useful for those who simply want to get all their pictures into some viewable form that won't yellow and fall apart in under twenty years. It is written, however, primarily for those who have greater goals for their memory albums. Place yourself in one of the categories below, and read the suggestions for how you personally can get the most out of this book.

## Experience and Interest Level

### Beginners

You have never done much about organizing your photos and mementos. You may have a lot of photos, but they are in shoeboxes, drawers, your mother's attic, and a few unknown locations. You have no idea why you might want to make sure the albums you buy are made from acid-free materials. You have decided that scrapbooking may be interesting, is probably important, and might even be fun.

Start with the front of the book and read through the end of Chapter 1. You can keep going straight through if you want, but if you are in a hurry to get started, skip to Chapter 3 to understand why the right materials are important, and then read Chapter 6. This will prevent you from damaging your memory items and help you avoid potential problems from the start. Then skip around to what interests you, and check the sources in the appendix if you don't know where to buy photo-safe scrapbooking supplies.

### Enthusiasts

You've been bitten by the bug! You already know a little (or a lot) about using materials that will last a long time. You have an album (or ten) done and you love this activity. From looking at the table of contents, you probably know just where to go. You have some idea where your knowledge is solid and where you would like more information. Be sure at some point to check out the Style section of Chapter 7. Many experienced scrapbookers have not yet considered what styles they like and how to apply them to their pages. This can make a big difference in letting your own personality shine through in the pages you create. It is also a good place to look if you ever get into a rut of doing the same type of pages all the time.

### Experts

You are a part of this new scrapbook industry or a dedicated family historian and have done your homework. Even at your level, you will find a lot of new information and twists on the tips you have already mastered.

You'll probably scan Chapter 3 to see if you agree with the semi-archival approach of this book. If you are selling scrapbooking supplies, Chapter 5 will help you market to the people who think this hobby is too difficult, time consuming, or expensive. If you teach people how to create memory albums, Chapters 5, 6, and 7 will help you refine your class content. Chapters 9-14 will give you ideas to use to keep students coming back for more.

## Explaining the Process

In addition to your experience with scrapbooking, consider how much you want to know about various methods of creating memory albums and the principles behind the guidelines. This book is written with a particular level of interest in the details of the scrapbooking process in mind. I've taken the liberty of offering some advice to three groups of readers based on the types of people I have encountered in the scrapbooking community.

Group one's motto is KISS: **K**eep **I**t **S**imple, **S**weetheart, please! One day a little boy asked his mom why water turned hard when they put it in the freezer, The mother suggested the boy go ask his father who was a professor of chemistry at the university. The reply she received was, "No thanks, Mom. I don't want to know that much about it." Parts of this book are going to explain more than some of you want know . That's okay; it's not necessary to read the whole book to use it. Be sure to read the Top Tips at the end of each chapter and read more where you are interested. If you will take the time to work through the projects in Chapter 7, you will learn a lot without having to put up with too much explanation, I promise.

Group two really wants to understand the scientific principles behind choosing photo-safe materials and the artistic process used to design great scrapbook pages. This is the level at which most of this book is written. It is designed to teach you enough to allow you to make informed decisions about your memory book albums, not to tell you what to do or buy. The design approach is one of learning basic skills and developing creativity, not giving you a model to copy. Most of the book will suit the style of these readers. Check the Top Tips on any chapters that do not interest you much.

My third group of readers wants it all. All the information, all the supplies, and all the details. The sources in the appendix, the Cyber-support information in Chapter 13, and the bibliography will assist those who want more detail than this book provides. In Chapter 3, and a few other places, you will be directed to additional scientific, technical, and professional resources. This book has a solid research base and is designed for family historians who want the basics and are not really interested in a lot of technical background. Practical principles that apply directly to choices of materials and techniques are the focus of the science covered here.

## Perspective

Early in my research, I sat for an hour while the presenter enthusiastically discussed the history of paper. After that class, I had a pretty good sense of when too much is too much. For those who do want more details, the references provided were carefully selected for their accuracy and good reputation in the conservation field as well as readability.

The tone of this book is decidedly informal. It also contains a lot of my own experiences and those of my family. Obviously, these are the people whose lives I have been documenting in my own albums, so I use them frequently as examples. If you are not fortunate enough to have an experienced scrapbooker to work with and ask questions, I hope this book can provide some of the support you need to learn this rewarding art. Imagine that we are together at your kitchen table, sharing ideas and suggestions. My approach is that of a casual chat with an informed friend. A little politics and experiences of a spiritual nature will pop up here and there. I believe those are important parts of the selves we reveal in our albums. Please translate any specifics to your own experiences and passions.

The information in this book has been checked and rechecked with various sources. It is not intended, however, to take the place of services of professional conservators, preservationists, or photographers. In many places this book will specifically direct you to seek the expertise of these professionals in certain situations. This book is intended to enrich your understanding of how to create a wonderful collection of memory albums. It will guide you in your decisions in buying materials and choosing processes. It will not make those decisions for you. More is being discovered about long-lasting album materials. Take advantage of the magazines and newsletters I suggest to keep yourself informed of the latest developments in archival science and product availability.

At the end of the book, in the appendix, you will find a long list of sources. This is the place to look to contact a company that offers the products discussed in the book. There is also an extensive glossary, so if you aren't sure what a term means in the context of scrapbooking, look it up there. You may have noticed that I use the terms "scrapbook," "memory album," "album" and even "book" interchangeably to describe the volumes you will create.

## CHAPTER 1

# Significance and Simplicity

### ❧ Why It's Worthwhile to Compile

For those of you considering creating a lasting collection of scrapbooks or memory albums for your family, your timing is perfect. The availability of supplies, ideas, and community support for this project is greater than it has ever been. Most prospective scrapbook makers are a little overwhelmed when they think about what will be required to arrange their photos in albums and add embellishments like journal entries and page decorations. This chapter offers some understanding of why the results are definitely worth the effort.

## What's New About This?

Thousands of Americans, especially women, are excited about the hobby industry's newest sensation: scrapbooks. But these books are not of the same species that my great-grandmother made or that you may have pasted together as a child. With these new albums, you can create a complete record of your personal history.

The enthusiasm for creating memory albums is growing for four reasons. To start, current scrapbook makers are seeking and choosing materials that will allow their albums to endure for generations, possibly even centuries. The research done by conservationists and archivists is now being used by consumers, who are demanding acid-free, long-lasting papers and stable adhesives, among other supply requirements.

Secondly, these scrapbooks are a sort of hybrid scrapbook/photo album. Photos are the intended focus for most pages, but concert tickets, report cards, and other memorabilia can be included as well. As people assemble these memory books, they are seeking to tell their own stories and those of their families. Journaling, or written information, about the people and events in the pictures is a very important part of this new breed of scrapbook.

Thirdly, the new scrapbooks have become an outlet for artistic creativity and a great excuse to play with scissors, craft punches, pretty paper, and stickers. For many designers, each page is a chance to create a little work of art. This is a big part of their interest and enjoyment. Others want interesting, cute, or beautiful pages, but they consider themselves to be artistically-impaired. Scrapbook suppliers have whole lines of paper and stickers marketed specifically toward this group. Many consumers are very interested in products that will give them "great pages with none of the work."

Lastly, these albums are different than the scrapbook collections of previous generations in the sheer scope of the project. How many photos do you have, or were ever even taken, of your great-grandparents? Probably one or two dozen at most. If they were photography or portrait enthusiasts, you might have one small album. Now jump forward to the generation of children growing up right now. It is not unusual for a family to have literally hundreds of photos of a five year old child. Most scrapbook makers and their family members fall somewhere between these two extremes in the size of their photo collections. Most families have enough photos to fill between half a dozen and two dozen albums. This is a significant project!

## What Are the Benefits of Doing All That Work?

Why would people assemble these detailed albums? The most universal reason is the desire to preserve their memories of special people and times in their lives. A second reason is their desire to send a message to their children and even later generations. When there has been a flood, a fire, or an earthquake, what possessions do people weep at losing? Again and again, the loss of the family photographs is regretted most. If the family (including the dog) is safe, the photo albums are what many will try to save.

This new type of scrapbook has captured people's imaginations and enthusiasm for several reasons. Obviously, if you are going to go to the trouble to make them, you want them to last. Many of us have an old album with black pages containing photos mounted with cellophane tape or rubber cement. The contents are usually badly yellowed, faded, and falling off the pages. If we think a scrapbook we make will look like that in a few years, why bother? With reason to believe our albums will survive in good condition for our grandchildren and even great-grandchildren to enjoy, we are much more motivated to take the time and effort required to assemble them.

In this book, several terms will be used interchangeably. "Scrapbooks", "memory albums", and "memory books" all refer to this new type of memorabilia collection. The term "photo album" will be used to refer to volumes that are designed primarily to hold photos. Some of these albums are made with a small space provided for writing a short caption for each photo. Otherwise, they are meant solely to display and store photos. Period.

As we'll discuss in the science chapter, today's photo albums are made of higher quality materials than the the photo albums of 5 or 10 years ago. What are the advantages to creating memory albums as opposed to simply getting all your pictures into photo albums? Some of the reasons are outlined above in the section on what makes these book different than scrapbooks of the past. Consider some of those benefits one at a time.

If you want your family albums to last a long time, there are conservation benefits to the new memory books. Manufacturers who focus on the new photo-safe scrapbook market are being educated by preservationists and informed consumers. As new evidence emerges concerning which materials will last the longest, the product lines of these companies will reflect those discoveries. For this reason, the quality of materials used in scrapbooks may be superior to those used in regular photo albums. Because the quality of photo albums is also improving, this is a relatively minor advantage. It is a consideration, however, especially in more economical and moderately-priced albums.

A much more significant advantage is the variety of documentation options the new scrapbooks offer to their creators. As this activity has grown in popularity, participants have searched for terms that accurately describe what it is all about. Most have settled into calling their albums "scrapbooks" or "memory albums." The term for people who create these books has not been firmly established. Some call themselves "scrapbookers," and the work they do "scrapbooking." To many marketers and manfacturers, scrapbooks are nothing more than the newest popular craft or hobby.

In Creative Memories literature, author and photographer Thomas Davies is quoted, "In this age of disposable everything, we must be careful not to dispose of our past. . .it is no small task to find, organize, restore, and preserve our photos, but if it is not done, a valuable legacy will be lost. We must establish a new tradition of the family photo-historian." These albums are about our family photographs, but they are not limited to that part of the story. Letters, telegrams, newspaper articles, and genealogy charts all have an important place in this new type of family album. My emphasis may be different from the person who compiles pages and pages of family-tree charts. My pages look very different from those of the person who has spent decades transcribing or typing her ancestors' journals. However, the basic purpose and intent are the same. We are family historians. Our albums record the histories of our families. Is this a hobby? Yes. Is it more than that? From my experience with those creating these magnificent family treasures, I say it most certainly is more than just a hobby. It is a special service to our families that is worth the time, effort, and expense required to do it. The role of family historian deserves respect and appreciation from those who will enjoy these albums and collections for many years.

In the type of albums you'll be taught to make in this book, the photos are important. However they do not and cannot adequtely tell the whole story you wish to convey. Among the half-dozen photos I have of my mother as a child is a photo of two little girls in Sunday dresses standing by a bird bath. It is a small photo that is faded and a little out of focus. Even if you knew my mother, you would probably not consider this photo very important. I have a much clearer, better photo of her taken when she was about the same age. When I came across this photo as I was redoing my heritage albums, however, I got very excited. I called my mother to make sure that what I suspected about this particular bird bath was true.

This photo was taken of my mother and her sister on the lawn of their grandmother's home. On more than one occasion, my mother had revealed her tomboy ways in the tales of her childhood. One of my favorites was the story of the bees. It reveals a carefree side of my mother that I seldom see. That bird bath in the photo is the same bird bath that her grandmother's neighbor's bees would visit to get a drink of water. My mother and my aunt would then push the bees into water. Of course the unfortunate bees would drown. To the girls' chagrin, Mr. McChesney the

bee-keeper always knew and reported the missing bees to their grandmother. In my album, the bees and bird bath story is mounted right under this photo. When my mother's grandchild reads this album, he has much more of a sense of that mischievous little girl than he could ever get from that faded photo alone.

My albums contain copies of newspaper clippings and telegrams that tell the story of my father during World War II. The postcards that his mother received months after he was shot down are such an important part of my family history. I look at the printing that says, "Nothing is to be written on this side except the date and signature of the sender. If anything else is added the postcard will be destroyed." I look at my grandmother's handwritten note, "Received March 26th, <u>4 months</u>." My father was shot down November 26, 1944. As I read these cards I get some vague sense of what it was like for that 21-year old pilot to be, in his words, "a guest of the German government" for half a year. I ache for his mother who had no direct word from him for four months after his plane went down. That part of my father's life, and war, is made real to me.

When my family looks at my albums they will have a chance to know me, even after I am no longer alive. They will read about my father becoming a prisoner of war. In my junior high album, they will see a section about a Navy officer, Commander Edward Martin. They will learn that for over two years I wore a bracelet that was inscribed with this man's name. He was a POW in Vietnam and a military support organization sold bracelets that listed the name of one of the many soldiers missing or being held prisoner in Vietnam. I purchased the bracelet and promised to wear it until the man came home. They will read of my joy when that war ended and I found Commander Martin's name on the list of men who returned home safely. The photo of him with his family that he sent when he answered my welcome home letter will have some meaning for them. My children and grandchildren will have a window into my life that I do not have with any of my grandparents. Yes, I have their photos, even some pictures of my grandparents when they were children. But I do not have their stories. Their joys and their pains are not recorded in my albums; only their likeness. I treasure what I have, but I long to know more.

These are some reasons why these new albums have such potential for preserving precious bits of our lives. Lists of items to include and hints on fleshing out the stories that your photos begin to tell are an important part of the "how-to" section of this book. If we think clearly about creating these albums, the emphasis will be on recording the important events, relationships, and feelings in our lives. The page decorations are important, but secondary.

## Simplicity

If you have looked at the albums of a scrapbook fanatic lately, it can make creating your own books daunting. (She has cute lettering with dots and bows, five colors of paper, stickers, stamped impressions, and even hand-traced pictures of bunnies on her pages. Who has the time, money, or talent to do all that?) Many people, if the sales of scrapbooking supplies are any indication! To close this chapter, I want to address the decoration and design issues of crafting these books. For myself, the design and page-cre-

ation is extremely satisfying. When my children were born, I found that taking half a day to do a drawing, or two or three days to do a painting, was just no longer a possibility. My artistic inclinations were used for a newsletter here, a seminar manual there, and occasionally just for doodles. Scrapbook pages gradually became manageable-sized art projects. A finished page took very little time, but was satisfying, due to my sense of accomplishment and the chance to experiment with color, form, and line.

For any other family historians who relish this activity as an artistic outlet, go to it! You deserve this. Make your pages as elaborate as you like. If you are criticised for the time or money involved, ask a few questions. How much is spent on the hobbies and sports of other family members? Is having these completed albums important to other family members? Will the rest of the family support your doing something that means so much to you? If you are being extravagant, set a scrapbook budget and stick to it. Sit down with your spouse or family and make sure they understand how important this is to you. There are women who overspend to support their scrapbooking habit, but most are carefully choosing the supplies needed to assemble their priceless family treasures.

If spending an hour to create one page sounds tedious and boring, know that scrapbooking does not have to be so time consuming. If you are designing elaborate pages for any reason other than just wanting to do it, stop. Beautiful, rewarding scrapbooks are sometimes very simple. The photos are there. Some special ones are matted to create emphasis. Some fancy paper or clip art may be included, and there is writing on every page. The stories are told, the materials are high quality that will last, and the experience of making the book was a joy. That is the bottom line for these precious keepsakes. If those three requirements are met, the process and the product will bring a unique satisfaction and enjoyment to the family historian and many family members for generations to come.

## CHAPTER 2

# Stories of Safe Scrapbooking

## ❧ Where This Trend Began

The photo album business was plugging along as it had been for the past 50 years until recently. Since 1994, however, the interest and demand for creative, long-lasting ways to store and display family photos has exploded. The beginnings of this growing field can be traced to a handful of individuals, two women's family albums, and a common passion for preserving family images and stories.

## Pioneers

In 1980, Marielen and Anthony Christensen exhibited over 50 volumes of memory books, housed in 8.5" x 11" type three-ring binders, at the World Conference on Records in Salt Lake City, Utah. These books were the result of years of compiling photos, memorabilia, family history narratives, and audio recordings that told the story of the Christensen family members. As a result of the popularity of their presentation, the family opened a business in Spanish Fork, Utah, to supply materials for making memory books. Mrs. Christensen gave lectures throughout Utah and the family published a book explaining and illustrating their approach to family albums. Other businesses in Utah were created to support the demand for supplies for these hybrid scrapbook-photo albums.

Jeanne English also had a small exhibit of her family history at the World Conference on Records. She discovered the importance of using long-lasting storage materials from her conversations with another exhibitor, Al Thelin. He was promoting acid-free supplies and making them available to individuals for the first time. Previously, companies such as his supplier, the Hollinger Corporation, had sold only to professionals and institutions. Mrs. English, with Deirdre Paulsen, also gave lectures and published *Preserving the Precious*®, a handbook on preserving family treasures in 1988. Their emphasis was on the use of archival materials that would ensure that albums and heirlooms would survive several generations in good condition. Their company, Restoration Source, offered archival albums, supplies, and products to preserve heirloom textiles, documents, and other precious keepsakes. They also hosted the first Archival Convention for memory book makers in 1997.

Dianne Hook of D.J. Inkers was one of the first artists to design specifically for the scrapbook maker. In 1992, a friend of hers, Brenda

Birrell, started Pebbles in My Pocket®, a small store offering a wide variety of clip art books, stationery by the sheet, stickers, colored card stock, die cut paper shapes, cutting tools and three-ring albums. Pebbles is now a large local retail, mail order, and wholesale business that has served as the model for many of the scrapbook stores that have opened in recent years. D.J. Inkers has expanded to offer several titles of clip art books, computer software, and idea books. Diane's whimsical designs are extremely popular with scrapbookers, and other companies have emulated her style in their scrapbook supplies.

## Creative Memories

While the interest in 8.5" x 11" format albums was snowballing in Utah, a very different type of album and company was experiencing increasing popularity across the US and later in Mexico, Canada, the UK and Australia. In 1987, businesswoman Cheryl Lightle and homemaker Rhonda Anderson founded Creative Memories® as a division of the Antioch Company. Their collaboration was inspired by an enthusiastic response to Anderson's presentation of her family scrapbook albums at a women's group meeting. The cornerstone of the enterprise was a commitment to preserving family history and the company's patented flex-hinge album for storing and displaying photos, memorabilia, and journal entries narrating a family's story. The Creative Memories albums had the same binding design as Webway albums sold in retail outlets. The page and page protector design, as well as the album cover materials, were unique to Creative Memories products.

Creative Memories is a direct sales company with, as of 1998, over 30,000 independent consultants. The company markets albums and a variety of supplies through classes taught by consultants in class coordinators' homes. The consultants also offer ongoing workshops to their customers. In the past year, users of Creative Memories products have been the target audience for other scrapbook manufacturers. The most popular Creative Memories album has a large 12" x 12" page size. In 1997, Hiller, Pioneer, and other album companies began marketing 12" x 12" scrapbook albums, and other companies started to produce paper and stickers for use in albums of this size.

## A Nationwide Trend

As businesses solely devoted to memory albums and preserving family treasures prospered, their suppliers took notice. Ellison Craft and Design, Mrs. Grossman's stickers, Sandylion stickers, Leeco, and Fiskars are just a few companies designing and marketing specifically to this growing segment of the craft industry. EK Success introduced the Zig Memory System pens specifically to meet the demand of the scrapbook consumer: archival inks that don't bleed. Late in 1997, several mass-market manufacturers finally began actively competing with the smaller album producers. Carr Albums, produced by the HB Group which makes Holson albums and Burnes of Boston products, are sold in three-ring and spiral-bound formats in Target stores. They also produce a scrapbook kit containing the acid-free supplies needed to assemble the memory album.

Some of these mass-marketers were careful to provide high quality supplies that meet sound preservation specifications. Others found acid-free papers of various qualities and quickly assembled kits to meet the demand for "archival" scrapbooks. Archival suppliers such as Light Impressions and University products also began marketing to scrapbook consumers. University created The Archival Company solely to serve the historian consumer market.

## Innovators

As the demand for supplies grew, so did the demand for information on how to create this new type of memory album. Hot Off The Press was one of the first companies to offer idea books, starting with Brigette Server's *Snip Your Snapshots, Trim Your Treasures* published in 1995. This book was created in association with the Fiskar company and Brigette used their paper edgers and other tools extensively in her designs. Since then, Hot Off The Press has added many idea book titles and a full line of scrapbook papers sold by the sheet and bound in booklet format. Several other companies published books illustrating the use of their products. In 1997, Stacey Julian and Terina Darcey self-published *Core Composition*, their innovative book on scrapbook page design, and Lindsay Ostrom brought out the *ABC's of Creative Lettering* published by EK Success. Lindsay's book won an award at the Hobby Industries Association's 1998 show. Interest in scrapbooking was evident at the convention and spaces in the workshops to teach retailers about this new hobby quickly sold out. The award for Best New Product went to the Crop-In-Style scrapbook supply carrying case. The Hobby Industries Association estimated that over $200 million were spent on scrapbook supplies in 1997 and expect that figure to rise.

*Memory Makers* magazine was founded by Michelle Gebrandt to assist, encourage and inspire scrapbook makers. Before starting the magazine, Michelle was a Creative Memories consultant and the first few issues of *Memory Makers* featured page designs that primarily used that company's products. Very little advertising was included. As more scrapbookers found out about the magazine, they began to include page designs that used supplies from many different sources and also to accept ads from several companies. In the fall of 1996, *Creating Keepsakes* magazine premiered. The most common page format featured in this publication was the 8.5" x 11" size, and the publication included a lot of advertising from the start. Several small businesses that produced memory album products quickly found out that an advertisement in *Creating Keepsakes* was an effective way to reach many buyers. Twice a year, the magazine includes a special Product Showcase section that serves much like a national yellow pages of available scrapbook supplies.

In 1997 the International Scrapbook Trade Association began publishing two newsletters: one for consumers, and one to serve the entrepreneurs of this new industry. Founder Jeanne Reed also sponsored The Great American Scrapbook Convention near Dallas, Texas. Memories Expo, with shows in Pomona, California, and Orlando, Florida, and the Scrapbook Expo offered conventions across the country exclusively for scrapbook enthusiasts. Several other conventions premiered in 1997 and may become annual events. Some of these also featured rubber stamps, a decoration supply used for scrapbook pages and paper crafts.

The DOTS (Dozens of Terrific Stamps) company began offering stamps by direct sales through its independent demonstrators. In 1997, they expanded their line to include scrapbook supplies under their Close to My Heart division. Though Creative Memories and DOTS remain the largest direct sales companies, Life and Times, Memories to Cherish, and other small entrepreneurs also make products available to people who want to start scrapbooking businesses of their own. On a larger scale, many companies offer the products of several scrapbook suppliers whole-sale, so small stores do not have to meet large minimum order requirements to be able to carry these items.

A most unique opportunity for scrapbook fans also started in 1997. Jennia Hart sponsored the first scrapbooking cruise. Jennia was also a pioneer in establishing the first scrapbooking Web site, The Scrapbooking Idea Network (www.scrapbooking.com), in November of 1996. By the beginning of 1998, over 100 existed. Some of these are small, non-commercial creations established just to share ideas and page layouts. Others, such as dMarie (www.dmarie.com), are thriving businesses that sell scrapbook products on-line while offering a wealth of information available at no cost via the Internet.

While large manufacturers are a growing presence in the scrapbook field, the pioneers of the industry are still vital voices. The Christensen's Keeping Memories Alive™ company now has over 70 employees, a large retail outlet, and a mail-order business with customers worldwide. They also sell wholesale, as do Restoration Source and Pebbles in My Pocket. Each of these companies and their founders contribute to the wide availability of information, albums, and scrapbooking supplies that provide the resources for anyone to create their own legacy of precious family albums.

**CHAPTER 3**

# Science of Safeguarding Memories

## ❧ How to Make Your Albums Last

### Green Veggies of Preservation

Photographs, paper, and memorabilia that make up the contents of memory albums are affected by several conditions which either prolong or shorten their lives. Unfortunately, the science of preserving photographs and documents is relatively young. The experts in this field still disagree on many issues because there is still a lot of research that must be done to determine the best materials to use to make our memory items last.

Disagreements exist as to which practices for preservation are best. But just as dietary experts with opposing ideas agree that green vegetables are healthy, there are a few principles which almost all preservation professionals agree are sound and reliable. Here are the "green veggies" of preserving your albums.

1. Keep items clean; avoid contact with dust, dirt, and skin oils.
2. Store items in the dark if possible. Avoid exposing them to strong light.
3. Avoid extremes of heat and humidity.
4. Keep photos and precious keepsakes away from direct contact with highly acidic materials and chemically active substances such as polyvinyl chloride, the plastic used on most three-ring notebooks.
5. Make sure all methods of mounting and storing original photographs and other valuable items are reversible. Examples of non-reversible methods include lamination, bronzing, and mounting with certain adhesives.
6. Use permanent, non-reactive inks for recording important information.

So the enemies of memory albums are dirt, heat and humidity, light, aggressive chemicals, irreversible mounting methods, and fade-prone inks. Light, water (humidity), and temperature change, especially heat, speed up chemical activity and deterioration in photographic images and paper.[1] Obviously, surrounding photos with active chemicals can also produce unwanted changes in the pictures. Being assured of the reversibility of the methods you use is important for many reasons. Most importantly, we are still learning how to make photos last as long as possible. If a page material is discovered to be harmful, or the page itself is damaged, the photo can easily be removed if the mounting method is reversible. Perhaps even more important is that these mountings make the photos easily available to copy using the latest technology. It is certainly possible to copy an entire album page, but it is very likely that you will want to be able to handle some of your mounted photos individually some time in the future. Notice that principles one and two are followed just by creating your album. Store the albums in the living areas of your home with proper dust protection and item three is also accomplished.

To address the last three principles, an overview of the component materials that are used in memory book construction is provided below. Discussion of product choice follows that section.

## Scrapbook Component Materials

### Paper

Paper is used as page material, decoration supply, and sometimes as a cover material in your album. The cardboard core of most albums is also a type of paper. Paper is usually made of wood pulp, cotton rag, or a combination of the two components. It is important for a family historian to know that there are four paper qualities to consider when choosing paper components for an album: pH level, lignin content, general construction, and color-fastness.

### PH Level

Old-fashioned cotton rag paper held up well over time. As the demand for paper increased, the components used to make it dropped in quality. Widely available wood pulp, which is quite acidic and deteriorates quickly, became the primary fiber source in paper. Alum and rosin sizings, bleaching agents, and some dyes made the paper even more acidic. Acids break down paper fibers through chemical reactions, making them brittle and discolored.

In case you slept through chemistry, here is a quick primer on pH levels as they apply to paper. Paper has a measurable pH level that indicates its degree of acidity or alkalinity. (Acidity is the capability of a substance to form hydrogen ions when dissolved in water.) It is a chemical reaction that can weaken the cellulose, "the backbone," of paper. Water is neutral, neither acidic nor high in alkalinity. It has a pH of seven. Anything over seven is alkaline, and anything below that is acidic. From 6 to 5 is a big jump. Paper with a pH level of 5 is 10 times as acidic as paper with a pH level of 6.

In the middle of the twentieth century, it was discovered that alkaline paper lasts longer than acidic paper. There were marked differences in papers produced at different mills. Some papers were stronger than others and took much longer to become brittle and yellowed. Since the component materials were the same, the variations were a bit of a mystery. Finally, William Barrow and other researchers tested the waters used in manufacture and found highly alkaline lime content in the water used to make the more durable paper. Even though cheap wood pulp was used, the water minerals buffered the paper and neutralized the acidic material so it did not break down as fast. [2] It works like an equation. You add alkalinity to acid items and the acidity drops toward neutral. Add acid to an alkaline item and the alkalinity is balanced out, moving again toward neutral. The alkaline minerals buffered the paper and protected it from its natural tendency toward acid deterioration. It was not until the late 1980s that paper deacidification became widespread.[3] Ellen McCrady, of Abbey Publications, and other individuals worked diligently to inform the preservation community and reform the paper manufacturing process.

Today, alkaline additives are carefully formulated to buffer paper and make it last longer. You can test paper pH levels with chemical pens. Chlorophenol red and Bromcresol green are chemicals that change color according to the acidity or alkalinity of the paper.[4] These pens are not infallible, but they are helpful for general family use. In my own experience, the Chlorophenol red type has proven to be particularly reliable as a portable test method. Sources for these pH test pens are included under Conservation Suppliers in the appendix. Too much alkalinity is also destructive to paper. In 1815, the unexpected result of using chlorine bleaching powder was that books actually crumbed to bits before they could be sold.[5] Researchers have accomplished a lot since then; surprises of that magnitude are unlikely to happen in the future. The nature of the raw materials used to make most paper today makes too much acidity the primary danger. We also live in a mildly acidic environment. Paper will tend to become more acidic over time just from exposure to the air.[6]

An acidic item can also damage photos and paper stored next to it. Acid migrates, or moves, from an acidic item to more alkaline items nearby.[7] A photo mounted on acidic paper, especially a fiber based, non-coated photo, will absorb some of the acid, and the paper backing will break down more quickly. The closer an item is to an acidic material, the greater the chance of chemical contamination. If an acid must travel through several layers of material to reach a photo, the danger is much less than when there is direct contact.

## Lignin Content

Lignin is a sneaky component of paper, the effects of which are still disputed. Some paper industry representatives still question the position that it speeds up the deterioration of paper. However, most paper and conservation experts now agree that lignin, which is a cell-wall material in plants, breaks down to acidic components over time. This chemical reaction is a major cause of yellowing in paper.[8] Paper bags and common corrugated box cardboard are made of high lignin papers. The tan color is due to the lignin. Some lignin will remain in any paper made from wood, but paper with 5% or less is considered to be lignin-free. Lignin content can be detected by testing with Phloroglucinol Grafts' C-Stain. Since this testing not practical for most consumers, and lignin only becomes acidic over time, it is important to buy from reputable paper suppliers. Contact Abbey Publications (the address is in the appendix) or check their Web site (palimpsest.stanford.edu/byorg/abbey), for a current list of available permanent papers.

## Paper Construction

Another consideration in choosing paper for your scrapbook is its construction. Papers with the same neutral or alkaline pH value vary widely in quality. An alkaline paper made of loosely pressed, poorly refined, highly buffered pulp is not going to last and stay attractive as long as a quality paper of the same pH level. By touching and bending papers, you can get a pretty good sense of their structure. If the paper is thin, cracks, or feels rough, it is not as durable as a thicker, more flexible stock with a fine finish. More scientifically stated, top quality papers have higher rag and alpha cellulose content and are free of groundwood, metal particles, waxes, plasticizers, or acidic sizings. By definition, recycled papers are composed of a mix of materials and chemicals. Due to technological advances in paper making, these papers can still be of a very high quality. Many preservationists, however, avoid recycled paper for important archival uses.

### Color-fastness

A final quality to evaluate applies only to colored papers: are they color-fast? This is quite simple to test with light and water. If the paper will be inside a memory book that is stored in the dark, light fading is a minor concern. The worst that will happen is that the paper will lose color a few years down the line. If you want to test for light, set a smaller piece of paper over the paper being tested in order to mask a part of the larger sheet. Set the paper on the dash of your car or in a sunny window area for a few days. Remove the masking item and notice whether or not fading has occurred.

The test for color fastness in moisture is even easier. Dip the paper in a light-colored bowl filled with water. Lay a bit of the paper on a wet, white paper towel. If the color bleeds, it could run in your albums. This is dangerous: it could dye the photos on the pages, especially those that are not coated with resin (usually older fiber based photos, pre-1970.) In case you are thinking that your albums will never be exposed to water, remember that accidents do happen. Areas flood, pipes burst, and albums do fall into puddles. If you live in a humid area, non-colorfast paper could transfer dyes to your photos simply from contact with the moisture in the air.

### Plastics

Three plastics that have been tested extensively and found to be safe to use around photos are: special polyester sold under the names Dupont Mylar D® and ICI Mellinex™ #516, polypropylene, and polyethylene.[9] This polyester is considered to be top quality for conservation uses and is recommended for encapsulating documents, a process described later in this chapter. It is extremely chemically stable and resists heat and cold. It is, however, prone to static cling. Most of the sheet protectors available today are made of polypropylene, though there are others still made from plastics that damage photos. This plastic is strong, clear and fairly stiff. Polyethylene is frequently used for storage sleeves for negatives. It is more flexible and more translucent than polypropylene. The flexibility allows for sliding negatives into a sleeve with less chance of scratching them. Henry Wilhelm disputes the safety of some products made from this plastic and claims that it may damage negatives.[10] It is important that the plastics not be coated on the surface that touches the photos and that they contain no additives. Clear plastics require a purer material and represent a more known quantity than non-glare sleeves.

Polyvinyl chloride, or PVC, is a chemically active plastic that accelerates the deterioration and fading of photos.[11] Have you ever opened a vinyl notebook filled with photocopied pages and had the front page stick to the binder? That is polyvinyl chloride at work. As this plastic deteriorates, it emits chloride gas, which combines with moisture in the air to produce very destructive hydrochloric acid. Many page protectors used to be made of this material, but customers disliked its tendency to lift the print from photocopies. PVC has a noticeable vinyl odor (like the smell of a new car) and will tend to stick to itself. All vinyl, including the naughahide used on the covers of many popular albums, are chemically active plastics that may damage photographs. Plastics touching photos directly have the strongest effect on them. Vinyl out-gasses, however, and can damage photos stored near them, out of direct contact. Climate plays an active role in this process. A humid environment facilitates the action of the gases emitted by vinyl.

Cellophane used for tapes and acetate used for older sheet protectors are also acidic and are plastics that should be avoided. Polyvinyl Acetate is considered to be stable as is polystyrene used by Kodak for slide carousels, cabinet dividers, and film spools. Most hard plastics are very stable and are safe for use around photos.

## Adhesives

For photo preservation use, we want adhesives that are stable, durable, and reversible. These are challenging criteria to meet. It is difficult to evaluate the effect of adhesives on the photos they touch or are placed beside. Many factors, such as other nearby materials and relative humidity, influence the deterioration of photographs in association with adhesives. Adhesives must be somewhat chemically active in order to stick. Many acrylic adhesives are very stable and are considered to be photosafe. Rubber cement, the adhesives used in most common tapes, and most glues are destructive to photographs.[12] In order for an adhesive to be a sound preservation supply, it must be completely reversible. The mounted item must be removable without its suffering damage. Many acceptable adhesives, including some glue sticks, can be reversed by applying a bit of water with a cotton swab to loosen the bond. Because it is so hard to predict exactly how an adhesive will behave 50 or 100 years from now, it is best to avoid direct contact of adhesives with photographs. With the resin-coated prints, there is a measure of safety built-in due to the backing. More vulnerable fiber-based prints are best mounted with corners, slits, and slip-in paper frames. With those prints in particular, liquid glues may indent the photos if they are applied directly to them.

Finding an adhesive product with a bond that holds as long as you leave it alone, but will lift if you need to remove the mounted item, is challenging. Generally, photographs and important documents are the main items that should be mounted only with reversible methods. If page decorations made of paper or stickers are permanently stuck to the page, that is usually acceptable. For those items, it is important to use adhesives that are chemically inert so that their presence on the page does not adversely affect the photos mounted nearby. The adhesives used to make stickers can effect photographs mounted on the same page. Mrs. Grossman's Paper Company has hired independent labs to perform the Photographic Activity Test (PAT) on all their stickers and they passed. They also publish data on the pH levels of the papers they use.[13] They admit, however, that they have only 18 years of experience with the longevity of their products. They do not know how they will perform 50 years from now, and they specifically recommend not adhering stickers directly to photographs.[14] It is unlikely that stickers of this quality placed near photographs will hasten their deterioration, but the appearance of the stickers themselves decades from now is another consideration.

One final factor to consider is pertinent to choosing adhesives and self-adhesive page decorations. The more chemicals used on a page, the more unpredictable the resulting chemical interactions and their effects on photographs will be. Limiting yourself to one or two adhesives on a page will cut down the likelihood of even more chemical activity than the individual items would create alone.

## Inks, Dyes, and Toners

Inks and dyes are used for writing and drawing on scrapbook pages. They are also present in stamped impressions, photocopies, computer print-outs, and colored papers that may be included in your books. Colorants in photos themselves will be addressed separately. With inks and dyes there are two primary considerations: 1) Will the substance itself cause the paper or photos on the pages to deteriorate more quickly? 2)Will the writing or drawing done with the ink last without fading over time?

One conservation mistake of massive proportion was the use of iron gall ink made from iron sulfate and oak galls. It was used from the 17th through the early 20th centuries. Even with the high quality, low-acid papers used during much of that time period, documents did not survive because the highly acidic iron gall ink eventually burned through the paper.[15] Although they may not be as bad as iron gall ink, most commonly used inks are chemically active, unstable, and non-permanent. Ball point ink and the inks in most felt tip pens will damage paper over time, will fade even in dark storage, and will run if they get wet. Ball-point pens also damage photos if they are used to write on the backs of the photos directly. The pressure used to write dents the photograph. Many children's markers are designed to wash right out of their clothing; these inks are not meant to last.

Pigment inks are more stable and permanent, in part because they do not interact very much with the paper.[16] Dye-based inks penetrate the paper, but pigment-based inks sit on its surface. In our albums we want as little chemical activity as possible. We want all the components to sit quietly and remain unchanged. The less interaction between the elements on a page, the more stable and enduring all those elements tend to remain. Most of the unwanted chemical reactions that happen in our memory books are partially caused by, or are accelerated by, water. Moisture in the air combines with chemicals on our pages, and things start to change. Pigment inks are desirable because they are impervious to water. All pigment-based inks are not of equal quality. Cheap pigments will fade or produce color shifts. This is the reason preservationists recommend black ink. It is made from a very stable pigment and also reproduces well. Using acid-free inks is important since acids lead to paper deterioration. Stable and non-reactive inks are also important because we want as little chemical activity as possible in our scrapbooks.

Carbon-based inks were also used when iron gall inks were common. They are as good as the iron gall ink was bad. Calligraphers and artists still use these inks today because they work well and are so stable. Most photocopiers today have carbon-based toners. The toner itself is very stable. How well the toner adheres to the paper can vary from machine to machine. You can test it by flicking the print with a fingernail and immersing the copy in water. These are not standard tests for permanence, but they will reveal how durable copies made on a particular machine will be over time. You can also test the adherence of the toner to the page by placing Scotch® Brand Magic Transparent tape on the print and lifting it off again. Higher quality copies leave no image on the tape.

Laser printers use heat to bond a very stable ink to the page and their images tend to be very permanent. If you are printing on cardstock, you may need to preheat the paper by "printing" a blank page and then running the paper through again immediately to make your printout. Acid levels vary in the inks used in ink-jet printers. Contact the manufacturer of your printer to find out the pH level of the inks in your machine. Even non-acidic ink-jet inks are not permanent.[17] They will fade and run if the printed image gets wet. Manufacturers are developing printer inks that will be more permanent.

Most colored cardstock contains non-colorfast and non-waterproof dyes. These dyes present a danger in the presence of water since they can bleed onto your photographs and discolor them. This is a particular concern with dark colors and fiber-based prints (usually pre-1970 photos with no resin coating.)

These are the basics of photo conservation. The next question is, how exactly do you follow these guidelines? How does this science lesson relate to buying supplies for memory albums? Most of the principles in the previous pages tell you what to avoid. You want to know what you can use. The following information will help you choose which materials to use in your albums.

# Preservation-Friendly Album Materials

## Albums

Choosing the album itself is one of the trickiest choices the family historian has to make. Most veteran scrapbook enthusiasts believe there is no perfect album available. There are, however, many extremely well-made and beautiful ones on the market. Even in the past few years, more choices have become available, most of which are much better for photo preservation than albums sold in the past.

## Acid-Free?

One of the controversies in the scrapbook field is the question as to how acidic an album can be and still be acceptable. As noted in our principles above, most experts agree that photos should not be in direct contact with acidic paper or other acidic materials. The controversy concerns the use of acid materials in other parts of the album, such as the core material of the covers or the edges of the pages. The other point of disagreement is whether it is preferable to use page materials with a neutral pH or to use pages that have been buffered, making them more alkaline.

Consider the use of acidic materials in album construction first. The reason that many well-made albums have core materials, and even covers, made of acidic material is that those materials are still more readily available than neutral or alkaline materials. There is no case for acidic materials being superior to neutral components. The question is whether or not acidic components hasten the deterioration of the photos significantly if the acid materials do not touch those photos directly. Completely acid-free albums, from core to cover materials, adhesives and all page components, are still hard to find. They are, however, definitely available. Album coverings made of vinyl or leather are also potential hazards to your photos. Again, the question is, if they do not touch the photos, how much damage do they do? A decision must be made based on current knowledge which we admit is incomplete. Until more album manufacturers submit their products for independent tests, we must make our decisions based on the information we have. Many well-made albums fall short of the completely acid-free criterion and still deserve consideration for some family album projects.

The question of neutral or buffered (alkaline) pages is more difficult to answer, because some experts believe that one will preserve photos better and other experts believe the opposite. Most of my research suggests avoiding placement of the emulsion side of photographs directly against highly alkaline surfaces.[18] Alkaline buffering is usually calcium carbonate. This chemical does not migrate as acid does. It remains fixed to the paper fibers that it coats. For this reason, it is only necessary to avoid direct contact between the buffered paper and the photo emulsion itself.[19] If buffered pages are used, page protectors or interleave papers should keep the front of the photos from touching the alkaline pages.

### Quality Structure

With all the "acid-free, no PVC emissions" claims plastered across even discount store albums, we sometime forget some common sense qualities we need in an album. It should be structurally well made. If the cover is going to tear or the spine construction break with in a few years of usage, it's a bad album. Some points to consider are the sturdiness of the page holders, the cover material, corner construction, and overall workmanship. If at all possible, choose albums that you have seen wear well over time. There are various types of ring, post, spiral, strap, and other types of page bindings.

With ring binders, look for the 'D' ring construction which allows the pages to lie flat against each other rather than curling around an 'O' ring. This design lessens the stress on the edges of the pages during storage, though it does make page turning a little awkward. Some conservators recommend ring binding for albums because the rigid structure supports the pages well. This cuts down on abrasion stress. Be sure the cover is large enough to protect the pages. From my experience with post-bound albums, I suggest shopping carefully for this type of construction. In some designs, there is so much stress on the material directly around the posts that they eventually tear. Quality is important in any metal used in your album. Cheap metal can rust or oxidize over time. If pages touch the metal, or the metal holds the pages in place, there can be problems.

Album size is mainly a matter of personal preference and what you need to accommodate your materials. There are, however, preservation concerns. For one, it is important to note that most conservators are horrified that people want paper memorabilia, photos and maybe even clippings together in one album. Managing acidic paper for inclusion in your albums is explained later in this chapter. If you choose to be very conservative, these items will need to go in separate albums. A less conservative but cautious approach is to place the paper items on pages and in page protectors separate from photographs. This choice needs to be made in order to plan your album purchases. Secondly, a smaller page will protect a fragile photograph better than a larger page. The smaller page is harder to bend and so physically gives more support to the photograph. Thicker pages or extra layers of paper in your page creation also provide additional support.

## Dust Protection

Consider an album's primary purpose: to protect and contain your pages. Since dust is an ever-present dirt danger to our photos, album construction that protects from dust is desirable. This is usually available in the form of a hard slipcase for the album or a cloth slipcover. As long as the album is made of completely acid-free and chemically-inert materials, the slipcase provides the best dust protection. If any album materials are chemically questionable, do not enclose your photos in contact with those chemicals. Use a slipcase only for top archival quality albums. A vinyl album in a slipcase is a preservation nightmare. In such cases, chloride gases are trapped in close proximity with the photos. An alternative that keeps out dust but does not contain the album materials as closely is a slipcover. They are not widely available, but are easy to make. Instructions for making one are in at the end of this chapter. More information is given in the storage section of this chapter, but a readily available slipcover that works for many albums is a well-laundered, clean cotton pillowcase.

## Page Protection

Generally, your best choice for page protectors are those made of polypropylene. This plastic is not as strong or as inert as Mylar D polyester, but it is easier to form into an effective page protector designs. Look for clear protectors that have no coatings added to the polypropylene. If you do not plan to store your albums inside a cabinet, and will not be using a slipcase or slipcover, consider using side-loading page protectors. They will not protect from dust as well as the other measures, but they are better than unprotected top-loading pockets. Dust settles on the top surfaces of items, which means that photos stored in top-loading page protectors in an uncovered album are very vulnerable to scratches and other damage from dust.

Make sure you don't use any old vinyl or acetate page protectors you may have around the house. If it has an odor, do not use it in your albums. Chemicals that reach your nose can also reach and effect your photos to varying degrees. Since scientists still do not know all the effects of polypropylene on photos, buy protectors made by companies actively involved in photo preservation. Office suppliers have switched from vinyl to polypropylene sheet protectors because they do not lift the print from copies. For some suppliers, that may be their only criteria. Suppliers serving conservationists and informed family historians will be monitoring their products with an eye toward better photo preservation. For example, we know that polypropylene coatings can be harmful to photos. Photo conservation conscious companies will be more likely to ensure they do not use materials that do damage photos in their page protectors.

### Lamination

Never laminate with common laminating machines, and avoid any lamination on valuable items such as photos. All lamination seals the surface that is laminated. This limits the item's ability to shift with environmental changes or "breathe." It also permanently traps surface dust and contaminants and seals the chemicals of the photo emulsion in a closed environment. If the photo was not rinsed well enough, lamination will speed up the damage done by the residual chemicals. Standard laminating machines also subject the object to high heat, and strong pressure that can cause it to age more quickly. Of course, this method is also non-reversible.

### Paper

For the highest level of preservation safety, choose acid-free, technically lignin-free, high quality, smooth, white, non-recycled, heavy paper. If you're thinking, "how boring!" I understand. Consider your goals for your albums. Consider choosing different goals for different albums. In chapter six, there are some options to help you choose what level of photo-safety you want for each of your albums. You can choose different levels of preservation standards for individual albums. The white paper ensures that no paper dyes will bleed onto your priceless photos.

Having so many high-quality, acid-free, lignin-free papers available, they are obvious choices for a quality album. The buffering question is still something to consider in regard to color photographs and albumen antique photographs. It is easy to find acid-free paper. It is much more difficult to find pH neutral papers. For photographs made prior to 1905, either make sure they are not albumen prints or mount them on neutral, non-buffered paper.[20] If you make sure the buffered paper does not touch the front of your color photos as discussed previously, the emulsion should be protected from alkaline chemicals. Low quality papers with a high lignin content may be highly buffered to make the papers acid-free. This cheap paper will quickly use up the buffering as the lignin deteriorates. This is the reason it is important to know the lignin-content of paper, as well as the pH level.

If you are storing your photos before placing them in albums, consider your storage materials for photo-safety as well. Especially if the photos or paper keepsakes will be stored for a few years, purchase lignin-free, acid-free boxes, folders, or envelopes. Safe plastics such as polypropylene are also acceptable for temporary storage. If you live in a humid climate, acid migration from storage materials should be considered. There are highly buffered acid-free storage boxes that do contain lignin. For short-term storage (less than a year) especially in dry climates, these present little danger to your photos. The manufacturers themselves state that these boxes are not intended for long-term archival storage. Scrapbook supplies such as mounting paper and, if they are used, stickers should be stored in a nonacidic environment if possible. Acid will migrate from low quality paper products, such a common corrugated cardboard boxes, to your alkaline paper. For short-term storage, this precaution may not be necessary.

## Mounting Supplies and Techniques

As noted above, for fiber-based prints, extra care is needed to mount them on the page. Their paper backing is much easier to damage than that of a modern resin-coated photo. For these photos and any other particularly special photographs or documents, use corners, slits, or other slip out methods. Photo corners should be made of acid-free, lignin-free paper or a safe plastic, not polyvinyl chloride. The corners should adhere to the page with a tested photo-safe adhesive, preferably one that has passed the P.A.T. Even with quality corners, take care not to damage the photo. It does put stress on the photo to bend it and remove it from the corners. For this reason, some conservators suggest using only three corners. This offends many scrapbook makers' sense of visual balance. I suggest getting all the copies of the photo you need before mounting it at all. Think through your needs so there is little chance you will have to remove the photo unless you are going to pull apart the whole page. In that case, cut the page away under the photo so it does not have to be bent. Obviously, this is most important with older photos that have already become brittle and are very likely to crack.

An economical, fully-reversible mounting method is to cut four slits in the page and slip the corners of the photo in them. This requires that you not crop the photo or that you leave corners. It also requires an album system in which each page is a separate sheet. Pages that slip into a page protector back-to-back will work with this technique.

Slip-in paper frames can be used to mount photos. Precut mats or mats cut with an craft knife or mat cutter may be used. Mount the frame on the page with a photo-safe adhesive on three edges (top, bottom, and one side works well). When the adhesive is set, slip the photo under the paper frame. This avoids bending the photo.

For resin-coated prints, more adhesives can be used safely and are still reversible without damaging the photograph. As a general rule, look for adhesives sold by reputable retailers specifically for use with photographs and preferably choose only those that have passed the current P.A.T. For mounting paper on paper, many glue sticks work well.

Avoid using rubber bands, paper clips, staples, and string, even for short-term photo storage. They put stress on the photos, can dent them, and the rubber will leave a residue.

## Pencils, Pens, and Print

### Ink

Inks need to be fade resistant, permanent, and non-reactive (this includes being acid-free). Pigment inks meet these standards. Be sure to avoid permanent pens not meant for paper and photo use. "Sharpie's" inks contain chemicals that will cause the ink to bleed. It will also yellow and harm your paper. These permanent pens are not even designed for marking on porous surfaces such as paper.

For important information, black ink is best. The pigment in black pens is time-tested, and stable.[21] Even with permanent inks, colors are more subject to fading than black ink. Reserve colors for decoration that is attractive but not essential to tell your stories.

### Computer Printouts

Printouts from laser printers are usually permanent and acid-free so they will tend to last and not damage your paper. Run the paper through the printer once by setting the computer to "print" a blank page. This will preheat the paper and cause the laser printing to adhere better, especially on cardstock. Some ink-jet printers use acid-free inks and some do not. Check with the manufacturer of your machine to be sure. Even if it is acid-free and will not chemically affect adjacent photos, ink-jet ink is not permanent. It will run if it gets wet and will fade faster than permanent inks. If it does run, it could dye the photos. Dot-matrix printers produce printouts that fade very quickly.

### Photocopies

Photocopies are usually safe to put in your books. Photocopy your acidic newspaper articles onto a creme or ivory acid-free paper such as Hammermill brand, to mimic the look of newsprint, and safely mount them in your books. The copies may not be permanent; some are subject to running and fading, but if you check your pages regularly, you will notice an item is beginning to fade and can copy it. Be sure to choose a copier that uses a toner containing carbon black pigment.

If you will be making a lot of photocopies for your albums, it is worthwhile to do a little testing on your own. Have an item photocopied at several copy shops and even on the different machines in one shop. Label each copy with the name of the shop and machine used to make it. Do the colorfast light and water tests on each one and check for print lifting with tape and scratching with a fingernail. These checks will allow you to make the best choice of the copy options you have available. The Kodak Ektaprint 85 system tested very well compared to other systems several years ago.[22]

### Adding Color

High-quality color pencils, chalks, and watercolors are relatively safe but are not permanent. Use them for decorating pages, but not for recording important information. If you use rubber stamps, use pigment inks. Heat embossing inks will tend to make the image last even longer.

### Photo Labeling

When writing directly on the back of a photo, use a soft pencil only on the edge. If you are determined to use a pen, the Pilot® Photographic Marker is a reasonable choice, but even this ink may transfer to a facing object or eventually migrate through the photo.[23] For these reasons, avoid stacking ink-marked prints and write only on the very edge. The Pilot pen may also be used to write on plastic enclosures, such as those used for negative storage. If you choose to trace template shapes on the front of a photo before cropping, use a soft Schwan All-Stabilo (blue & white) pencil. These will wipe off the photo front with a soft cotton rag. The white will not mar white album pages if the bits drop on the page.

# Page Decoration

## Clip Arts, Stamped Images, and Color

Photocopied clip art is very safe and looks very appropriate in books of older photos. Dover Publications books are an excellent source of copyright-free borders and pictures. The books are available at many book stores and their address is in the appendix. Images can also be traced onto a lightly colored page with a pigment ink pen. Place the art on a light box. Place the page over the art and anchor it in place. Trace the image with a pen directly, or do so first with a pencil and then retrace with a pen. Computer clip art printed out on a laser printer is also very long-lasting.

Rubber stamped images made with pigment inks and heat set or embossed are permanent and photo-safe.[24] Most embossing powders are made from nylon, an inert material. You may also safely use pigment ink pens, quality colored pencils, and chalks.

## Stickers

Strict archival standards suggest limiting the amount and number of chemicals that come in contact with, and even in close proximity to, photos. Stickers are still a fairly unknown element for long-term use. For a less conservative but reasonably safe approach, make sure stickers are made from acid-free, lignin-free paper, safe non-reactive inks, and stable adhesives. Using only stickers that have passed the P.A.T. is also a good precaution.

## Paper Decorations

Avoid die-cuts from non-colorfast paper to prevent the possibility of dying photos should the book be exposed to water. A reasonable standard of safety allows die-cuts made from paper that meets the standards mentioned previously. Take extra care with fiber based prints. Note: all shiny metallic and "homemade" (rough with flower petals, grass, etc.) papers I have found tested acidic with a pH pen, even though scrapbook store employees told me several of these papers were acid-free. Acid-free paper of this type may become available, but check carefully before using it.

Dry embossing and paper cutting from light-colored or colorfast paper are two very archivally sound methods for decorating pages. Punching shapes and cutting with decorative paper edgers is photo-safe if the paper is acid-free, lignin-free and colorfast.

## Cropping

Cropping is a decorative technique that still must be evaluated for its long term effect on photographs. The hard and fast rule is to refrain from cutting modern Polaroid prints such as TZ, 600, Spectra, and Captiva. These prints retain developing chemicals in their finished state. Cutting them may expose the photo and the surrounding page to chemical degradation. Mount these prints and place a decorative cutout frame-type mat over them. According to a Polaroid representative, older peel-away Polaroid prints may be cropped without creating the chemical problem.[25]

The primary reason to avoid cropping any print is that you crop out historical information. If you are attentive to this danger, you can make your own cropping decisions. With forethought, you will probably not make choices you will later regret. The secondary reason not to crop involves the deterioration of the photo itself. When you leave a border when a print is developed, pollutants in the air will attack that exposed blank edge. The image itself gets a measure of protection from the border.[26] Think of older photos you have seen that are yellowed. Frequently the edges look worst and are usually the part of the photo that gets skin oil on it when the print is handled. Since you usually crop a photo and then mount it in an album, this is less of a concern. Again, this is an area where you will need to weigh the benefits of cropping with the costs to the photo.

## Principles Are Important

A brief note of explanation is in order. Some readers may wish this chapter consisted only of a list of photo-safe products. Ten or twenty years from now, that might be appropriate. But there are still a lot of photo preservation issues that require much more research. At this time, even the most diligent photo preservation scientists do not have definitive answers as to the best materials to use to make your photos last, or they do not have answers you would like. Scrapbook store owner Kim Cook was researching this subject and called a local university with very knowledgeable conservators. Their helpful reply was the suggestion to place her photos in acid-free envelopes and store them in a metal box in a cold, dry environment. Now doesn't that sound like fun?

Steven Puglia, Preservation and Imaging Specialist at the National Archives in College Park, Maryland, has researched the issue of whether or not museums should copy or just carefully store valuable photographs and negatives. His recommendation for most institutions is a combination of both approaches. The factors he urges conservators to consider are the value of the items, size of the collection, type of photographic materials, desired use of the collection, and budget available for the project.[27] This is exactly what the family historian must consider. This chapter is designed to help you become an informed consumer and family conservator so you can make your own decisions. No one knows your collection like you do. José Orraca, professional conservator, says, "First a conservator must have love and respect for the work of art."[28] The personal importance of your photographic collection makes you uniquely qualified to choose the materials and methods you will use to display it and make it last. The principles you need to understand are very basic.

When you understand the basic principles, and know what questions to ask, you will be able to make your best choices. Product availability in this area changes daily. With the information in this chapter, you will be able to evaluate products as they come on the market. You will also be able to choose the level of preservation in conjunction with your other goals. The availability of your albums to your family and design considerations must be evaluated along with preservation principles. Product choices are important, but proper storage and handling is just as vital to preservation.

# Habits, Storage and Copy Options

## Work Habits and Handling Albums

For special photos, consider wearing cotton gloves when cropping them and placing them in albums to avoid fingerprints. At the very least, wipe off visible fingerprints gently with a non-scratch cloth such as an old, soft, cotton t-shirt. Wash your hands before working on your albums. Keep crumbs and drinks away from albums to prevent damage and attracting insects.

Handle albums gently. Support them well, especially at vulnerable points like the bindings and page corners. Avoid flexing, or bending pages and especially the photographs themselves.

## Storage

Remember, the worst dangers to your photos are light, dust, heat, and water (humidity and flood damage). Acid from skin oils and poor-quality album materials are secondary to these primary dangers. To prevent the worst, store your albums:

A. In the dark
B. Protected from dust
C. At a reasonably constant temperature comfortable for people
D. Away from water hazards such as water pipes and leaky rooms

Ideally, albums would be kept at a comfortably cool 65-68 degrees Fahrenheit. Chemical activity doubles with every 10 degrees increase in temperature.[29] It is not necessary to build a special room to store your scrapbooks. Choose a cooler location rather than a warmer one if you have storage areas with different temperatures. Relative humidity should be below 60 percent to avoid mold and water stains and above 25 percent to prevent cracking and curling of photos, as they loose water content to the dry air.[30] If relative humidity goes above 80 percent, the photos may stick to plastic sheet protectors. The level of humidity is also a factor in how other conservation practices will affect your photos. Drier air permits less chemical activity. Residents of Colorado can be less cautious with conservation and their photos will still last longer than those of a very conscientious humidity-smitten Floridian. It may not be fair, but it is a factor in making preservation choices. Silica gel canisters are available from preservation suppliers to absorb some of the humidity in the storage area. Because humidity is so damaging to your photos, consider using these canisters if you live in an extremely damp climate.

Stagnant air should also be avoided to prevent fungus problems, especially in areas with high humidity. Cycling, or temperature and humidity changes also damages photos. (It should be obvious that most basements and attics are the worst places to store photos.) Exterior walls also tend to change temperature more than inside walls and should be avoided.[31]

In regard to temperature changes, be careful not to take albums from very cold storage into a very warm place. An album that has been in a car in freezing weather for several hours must be warmed slowly. This will avoid condensation of water vapor from the air forming on the photos. Any plans for truly cold storage of photo materials must be made carefully and include some type of moisture protection. Read the instructions that accompany cold storage containers and consult an expert before freezing photographic materials.

One of the best places to store albums is in your linen closet (assuming it is not in a bathroom with a shower or under the path of water pipes). This provides much better dust and light protection than open bookshelves. The shelves also tend to be spaced widely apart so that even a tall album can be stored upright. If an album is structurally sound, store it upright to protect the photos from the pressure of the weight of the whole album. This can limit scratches and cracking on older photos that are already brittle. If the album itself is unstable, it may need to be stored flat. Slipcases provide extra support and dust protection for your albums. If they are used, albums may be stored on open shelves.

Another option is to store albums on a metal utility shelf placed inside a clothes closet. The metal is inert and chemically inactive. If you store albums on wooden shelves, be sure they are sealed with polyurethane or a water-based acrylic paint. One note about fresh paint: it can be very harmful to your photos. Photos in frames left in a room painted with oil based paint have faded noticeably overnight.[32] Remove all photos from any areas to be painted. Take them to a friend's house. Acrylic paint is fine after it is fully dry. Keep all photos out of rooms freshly painted with oil-based paint for 4-6 weeks. Photos should also not be stored near laser printers or photocopiers because of damaging ozone emissions.

## Negatives and Copy Options

### Negatives

Experts say your negatives will probably outlast your prints, so take good care of them and have copy negatives made of the photos you consider most important. ("Best" photo of each ancestor, any personal favorites, and a small special collection of photos of your immediate family is a good start).

Store your negatives separately from your scrapbooks. In case of a disaster, only one set would be damaged. Fire safes may protect negatives from smoke damage, but they will not withstand severe heat. If it is possible, store your negatives in another location such as a relative's home or a bank safe deposit box. Use safe plastic enclosures or archival paper envelopes to store your negatives. Buffered paper is best for black and white negatives and unbuffered for color.[33]If you place more than one negative in a sleeve, they may scratch each other. Check any negatives you have that were made before 1945 to see if they are labeled "safety film." If they are, store them as described. If not, take them to a photo lab. Nitrate film is flammable and can self-combust. Have copies made of any nitrate negatives and then dispose of them.

Copies made from copy negatives will lose quality in comparison with the original. The lights will get lighter and darks darker, making the contrasts stronger and loosing some subtle values in the photo. This is the only method that gives you a negative for future use. If you need several copies of a photo, it may be your best option. The negative itself is expensive, but the prints are not, so the cost averaged over several copies will be low per print. Also, the original photo will be exposed to strong light only once (when the negative is made).

## Print-to-Print

Other options will give a better quality copy. The Kodak® Image Magic CopyPrint system creates a print made directly from your print and is a digital image. If you look closely, you may be able to see the dots that make up the image. A higher quality, longer-lasting print-to-print system is the Fuji Pictrostat process.

If you have ultra-sound photos, and want to include them in your album, get them copied as soon as possible. Those images are extremely unstable and will fade significantly in just a few years.

## Laser Copies

Less durable, but good quality, economical copies, are made with the laser color copy process available at your copy shop. The images are clear and long-lasting. Be sure the copies are made on acid-free paper and aren't exposed to extreme heat. The color copy image can melt and shift in heat. If you are doing a lot of color copies, shop around. Take the same photo to several shops and compare quality. There is frequently a wide range of results in quality due to operator expertise and the machines used.

Consider making a child-proof color copy album of precious photos. This allows even tiny children to enjoy photos of their ancestors while protecting the original prints. Choose your copying process carefully. Repeated exposure to bright light from copiers and camera flash will accelerate fading. Decide how many copies you will probably need in your life before choosing your copy methods. You may want to take the extra precaution of using a piece of Acrylite OP/3 plastic to protect your photos from the bright light while you copy them. This 1/4" thick sheet will block the light rays, while permitting the machine to capture a clear image.

## Digital Reproduction

The final copying issue to consider is a unique option only recently available. All the copy processes described above result in some loss of quality with each generation of copy made. You have seen a copy of a copy of a copy. It is usually not a pretty sight. Also, all the products resulting from the processes above, including the negatives, are known to deteriorate over time. Digital copies, however, are unique because they can potentially keep an image unchanged for centuries.

The digital copy is stored on a disk or, for more durable storage, on a CD-ROM. A CD will not last for hundreds of years[34]. However, if the information on the CD is copied onto a new CD, or some future storage technology, before the CD deteriorates, the images lose no quality at all. A photo taken in 1998 and stored on a CD should be able to be printed out in original condition in 2998 if the proper care is taken. As technology progresses, a truly permanent storage method may be developed before the present CDs require recopying. Consider having copies of your most precious photos, or album pages, stored on CDs. The computer resources chapter describes this option as well.

## Choices in Film and Photo Processing

### Photographic Papers and Film

Henry Wilhelm strongly encourages choosing your photo processing and film with care. In his book, *The Permanence and Care of Color Photographs*, Wilhelm reports that photographs printed on Fujicolor Super FA Type 3 paper and Fujicolor Supreme SFA3 paper remained unfaded much longer than those printed on Kodak papers.[35] He states that mass-market portraits may last longer than expensive professional portraits due to the papers used to print the pictures.[36] He also recommends Fuji Super G 200, Konica Color Super SR 200, 3M ScotchColor 200, and Polaroid OneFilm Color 200 over Kodak's ISO 200 films for general consumer use.[37] My research indicates that the primary factor in print longevity is whether or not the prints are displayed.

All films made in the last few years are of exceptional quality in comparison to the color films of the 50s, 60s, and 70s. Photos stored in dark places, such as memory albums, will not show the variation of the prints displayed in frames. Even so, the tests of photos printed on different brands of papers reflect a definite difference in quality between materials exposed to the same conditions. If the longer lasting product is available and reasonably priced, it makes sense to take that advantage in preserving your memories. Fuji has recently introduced a Crystal paper that accelerated aging tests show may maintain image quality for 200 years.

Take care of your film as carefully as you do your finished prints. Keep film cool and especially avoid leaving film or your camera in a hot car. When you purchase film, check the expiration date and get the freshest film that you can.

### Film Processing

Borge Andersen, owner of a preservation-oriented photography lab for 30 years, recommends carefully choosing your photo processor and inquiring about the lab's rinsing procedures.[38] For labs to complete film finishing in one hour, short-cuts may be made somewhere. The only step during which time can be cut is the rinsing process. When short-cuts are taken, it is much more likely that residual processing chemicals will be left on the prints. Negatives may also be rinsed for too short a time to remove all chemical residues. These chemical residues have been proven to speed up the deterioration of the finished prints.[39]

Inquire about the processing times at the photo finishing businesses near your home. If you go through a large retailer, you may need to get a phone number and call the lab they use. You may also ask if they process following the recommendations of the film manufacturers. All major photographic material companies send detailed specifications as to times and processes for different films and the chemicals used. Improper time in the chemicals, or use of stale chemicals, will result in inferior photos. For slide processing, Kodak even has a quality assurance program called the Kodak Q lab program. Participating labs are regularly checked for quality and methods, and are dropped from the program if their work is not up to Kodak's standards. Ask your processor if they coat the negatives. This is undesirable and may shorten their useful life.

Because they are so economical, you may have most of your film processed at a local retail outlet. Avoid one-hour processing unless you know the lab you use rinses the photos sufficiently. Consider occasionally taking your film to a top quality lab. Each year, choose one or two rolls of special photos to give special treatment.

## APS and Air Travel

APS, Advanced Photo System, is still a very new process. Before using this type of photos exclusively, wait a few years. If you have an APS camera, take at least some photos each year with a conventional camera.

Air travel presents a danger to unexposed film. The x-ray machines used to inspect carry-on luggage can fog your film and the effects of radiation are cumulative. For best protection, carry film in a lead bag and ask for hand inspection. Unless you use very low speed films, have an APS camera, or travel to some foreign airports such as Cairo, you may not need to worry about this. Walk-through and wand metal detectors will not hurt your film, but will damage audio and video tapes.[40]

# Other Album Keepsakes

## Newspaper Clippings and Documents

Newspaper clippings, certificates, and other special papers present a special preservation challenge. If you are very fortunate, the paper item is fairly new and printed on acid-free paper. This can be checked with a pH test pen. The pen leaves a permanent mark, so use it on an inconspicuous spot on the document. If it is acid-free, it can be mounted on a page using photo-safe mounting methods. Since paper will tear if it is pulled from most adhesives, make sure you mount the item with corners, slits, or a fully reversible adhesive if there is any chance it will need to be removed from the page.

## Copies and Deacidification

If the item is acidic newsprint, consider photocopying it using a high-quality machine and acid-free paper. The original can then be stored in an acid-free box with buffered paper or discarded. If you want to treat the acidic paper item to prolong its life, there are two very good options; for the longest preservation, use both. The least expensive method is to rinse the item in a pan of distilled water with one drop of detergent added to break the surface tension of the water. If the water gets very yellow, discard and rinse again in fresh water. To protect the paper from tearing while it is wet and weakened, you may use a clean piece of nylon screen material to support the paper as you rinse it. Allow the rinsed item to dry completely on a flat surface.

The second method can be done after the rinsed paper is completely dry or without having rinsed the paper at all. Spray the back side of the item with a deacidification spray. Wei T'o is one such spray which has been used by the Library of Congress for many years. It must be sprayed outside and has a short shelf life. It should also be stored upside down. Gather many items to treat at one time, (one can will treat approximately 25-50 pages), or buy a can with some friends in order to use it up quickly.

Bookkeeper spray has a longer shelf life, is more environmentally friendly, and has less tendency to clog the nozzle. Either spray should be sprayed on the back side of the item until it is damp enough to darken slightly in color. Do not saturate the item. The buffering agents in the spray will stop the acidic activity of the paper and keep it at an alkaline or neutral level for many years. The initial acidity of the paper and the specifics of the buffering process and the environment will effect how quickly the paper becomes acidic again. If it is rinsed first, it will last longer. Before using either of these methods, make a high-quality photocopy of the document first and then test the print or ink for water resistance. The sprays come in different formulas, some of which are designed for use on documents that have inks that may run. Test inks with a cotton swab before spraying the entire document. Homemade milk of magnesia solutions contain extra ingredients and may not be as effective as the commercial sprays.

### Encapsulation

If you want to give a special document extra protection, you may encapsulate it. You will need two pieces of Mylar D® or Mellinex™ polyester cut large enough to overlap the document's edges by at least 1/2". You can enclose the document in one of two ways. Sew the document in, using nylon thread and a zig-zag stitch all around. For longest paper life, air needs to circulate around the document. Air can get in through the stitching, but you may also leave a small 1/4 inch gap unsewn. You can also seal the pouch with Scotch Brand #415 double-side tape. This is also available from conservation suppliers. Adhere the tape at the edge of one piece of the plastic, leaving a small gap that will not be sealed. This allows air to circulate and avoids trapping chemicals in the encapsulation. Make sure the document has at least 1/4" space all around its edges to keep it from touching the tape. Place the document in the middle of the plastic, remove the paper backing from the tape and carefully place the top piece of plastic over the document. Burnish the tape down to seal. Do not encapsulate acidic documents that have not been treated to reduce the acid content. Charcoal and pastel drawings also should not be encapsulated because the static charge of the polyester will lift the particles from the paper. The encapsulated document can be mounted on a scrapbook page or slipped into a page protector which allows both sides to be viewed.

## Photos Trapped in Old Albums and Other Disasters

### Self-Stick "Magnetic" Albums

Now you understand how to properly care for your photos. The only problem is that a lot of those photos are stuck in old self-stick "magnetic" albums. What now? Proceed carefully. If the photos are stuck fast and are very important to you, consider copying at least some of them using one of the print-to-print method before you do anything else. Just remove the pages from the album, cut the pages out if it is spiral bound, and take the page to the copy business. Remove the plastic cover sheet and make copies with the photos still stuck on the page. When you are ready to remove them, take your time and work carefully.

Take a flat plastic object (such as an icing spreader) and see if you can ease it under the photos. If so, work around the edges and lift them off keeping the print as flat as possible in the process. If that does not work well, try working dental floss under them to lift them off. Finally, if the adhesive still holds fast, warm it as little as necessary to loosen it with a blow dryer. Freezing can also make the adhesive let go but must be done cautiously to avoid water damage due to condensation when photos are removed from the cold. Seal the album in at least two airtight bags before placing in the freezer. Allow the album to warm up before opening the bags, but try to remove the photos while it is still slightly cool.

If the photos are very valuable, and if these methods fail, seek professional help from a conservator or photo lab. For any photo damage work, professional help is usually well worth the cost. If your albums ever get water-soaked in an accident, call a professional immediately. Keeping the photos wet or freezing them are ways to minimize the damage, but both methods can damage the photos further if they are not done correctly.

# Dirty And Damaged Photos and Memorabilia

## Cleaning Photographs

Wipe any fresh fingerprints off the front of photos immediately with a soft cloth like an old clean cotton t-shirt. Do not use facial tissues because their fibers can leave fine scratches on the photo emulsion. PEC®-12 photo and slide cleaner is available from photography and archival products suppliers. It can be used to clean older skin oil and residues from photos. If you have items that are dusty, use a camel hair brush to gently whisk the particles away. Consider getting a small container of canned air to blow away dirt if you have a very large collection of photos or papers that are very dusty.

## Curled Photographs

Curled photos may be flattened without damaging them if you protect the emulsion layer that may be brittle. If the photos are flexible and curled only slightly, try placing them between sheets of acid-free, unbuffered paper with books or another heavy weight on top. If they are stiff and severely curled, you need to moisten them in order to avoid cracking the emulsion layer when you flatten them. Lightly spray the back of the photo with distilled water and let it sit for a few minutes to allow the water to penetrate. Then place the photos between paper and weight them as described. Even this method may cause cracking, so do one or two photos and check the results after two or three days before working on a large set. If cracking occurs, consult a conservationist for other options to treat the problem.

## Cleaning and Repairing Paper

Dirt and marks can sometimes be removed from paper by rubbing them gently with grated bits of an ordinary eraser. By rubbing only with the tiny pieces, you may be able to lift the marks without putting too much stress on fragile paper. Since most older paper has become quite brittle, it is important to use extra care not to tear it. If a document is torn, it can be carefully repaired with document tape available from archival suppliers. Do not use regular transparent tape for these repairs. Frequently, you can align the edges of the tear and apply tape to the back side only. If the document will be mounted in an album, the repair may make the tear almost invisible.

## Choosing Supplies

As you know by now, many companies recognize that scrapbook supplies are becoming very popular. For this reason, many manufacturers are rushing to fill the need. Some of these businesses are doing their research carefully and creating top quality products that meet preservation standards described in this chapter. Other companies are cutting corners, seeking the cheapest materials that can be called acid-free, and selling inferior products.

### Suppliers and Stores

The guidelines for choosing a supplier are simple: Seek well-informed individuals who are personally concerned with providing truly photo-safe scrapbook supplies. If you choose your retailers well, they will be a great help in finding quality supplies. It is still important to check on materials yourself on occasion, but if you know the store owner or buyer is well-informed, you will have less work in this area.

### Manufacturers

Look for companies that: 1) Submit their products for independent analysis and testing, especially the P.A.T. (Photographic Activity Test) and are happy to provide you with a copy of the results. 2) Disclose the exact materials used in their products and the manufacturers of any raw materials such as paper. 3) Produce their products in the U.S., Canada, or Europe. At this time, the degree of control a company can exercise over items produced in many other countries is minimal. Unless they have this control, a company can't guarantee uniform quality and consistent use of appropriate raw materials in the finished supplies.

### Choices

This is an important project. If consumers demand quality and support businesses that provide it, manufacturers will meet the need by creating well made supplies. Be sure to patronize the small scrapbook stores and mail-order companies. These businesses are the reason you can buy individual die-cut shapes and beautiful stationery papers by the sheet. If you give all your business to mass-market stores as they jump on the scrapbook bandwagon, the variety, quality, and personal service provided by these small entrepreneurs will disappear. Buy things on sale and buy expensive items from large chain stores if you need to, but value the time and expertise of the small store owners and buy what you can from them. If individuals such as Jeanne English and Deirdre Paulsen of Restoration Source, Ellen McCrady of Abbey Publications, and photographer Al Thelin had not championed the cause of making archival-quality materials available to consumers, scrapbook supplies would be of a much lower quality today.

# End Notes for Chapter 3

1. Laurence E. Keefe, **The Life of a Photograph,** Butterworth Publishers, Woburn, MA, 1984, p. 231.
2. Laurence E. Keefe, see note 1, p. 85.
3. Utah State Archives and Records Service, "How to Handle Record Materials, Preservation Leaflet #3," Salt Lake City, UT, March 1996.
4. Ellen McCrady, "pH Pens and Chlorophenol Red," **Alkaline Paper Advocate**, Abbey Publications, Austin, TX, July 1995.
5. Ellen McCrady, "The Nature of Permanence," **North American Permanent Papers**, Abbey Publications, Austin, TX, 1997.
6. Laurence E. Keefe, see note 1, p. 85.
7. Craig A. Tuttle, **An Ounce of Preservation**, Rainbow Books, Inc., Highland, FL, 1995, p. 33.
8. Ellen McCrady, "Lignin on Trial," **Abbey Newsletter**, Abbey Publications, Austin, TX, July 1994.
9. Anita Young Hallman, **Self Preservation**, Deseret Book, Salt Lake City, UT, 1997, p. 234.
10. Henry Wilhelm, **The Permanence and Care of Color Photographs**, Preservation Publishing Company, Grinnell, IA, 1993, p. 497.
11. Laurence E. Keefe, see note 1, p. 248.
12. Henry Wilhelm, see note 10, p. 369.
13. Mrs. Grossman's Paper Company, Facts, Fiction, and Fun; Petaluma, CA, 1997, p. 6.
14. Mrs. Grossman's Paper Company, see note 13, p. 3.
15. Craig A. Tuttle, see note 7, p. 20.
16. Jeff Winston and David K. Platt, National Stampagraphic/Clearsnap, Inc., Anacortes, WA, 1997
17. Anita Young Hallman, see note 9, p. 199.
18. Helen D. Burgess and Carolyn G. Leckie "Evaluation of Paper Products: With Special Reference to Use With Photographic Materials," **Topics in Photographic Preservation - Volume Four** (compiled by Robin E. Siegel), Photographic Materials Group of the American Institute for Conservation, 1991, p. 100.
19. Helen D. Burgess and Carolyn G. Leckie, see note 18, p. 100.
20. Helen D. Burgess and Carolyn G. Leckie, see note 18, p. 100.
21. Craig A. Tuttle, see note 7, p. 20.
22. Ellen McCrady, ed., "Literature," **Abbey Newsletter**, Abbey Publications, Austin, TX, April 1995.
23. Henry Wilhelm, see note 10, p. 369.
24. Embossing heat-seals inert nylon over stable pigment ink, so the results are very long lasting.
25. E-Mail message from the Polaroid company, January 1998.
26. Henry Wilhelm, see note 10, p. 441.
27. Steven T. Puglia, "Negative Duplication: Evaluating the Reproduction Needs of Collections," **Topics in Photographic Preservation - Volume Three** (compiled by Robin E. Siegel), Photographic Materials Group of the American Institute for Conservation, 1989, pp. 124-125.
28. José Orraca, "Developing Treatment Criteria in the Conservation of Photographs," **Topics in Photographic Preservation - Volume Four** (compiled by Robin E. Siegel), Photographic Materials Group of the American Institute for Conservation, 1991, p. 100.
29. Laurence E. Keefe, see note 1, p. 231.
30. Laurence E. Keefe, see note 1, p. 231.
31. Craig A. Tuttle, see note 7, p. 51.
32. Anita Young Hallman, see note 9, p. 111.
33. Anita Young Hallman, see note 9, p. 111
34. Michael Guncheon, "Helpline Column," **PC Photo**, Los Angeles, CA, November 1997.
35. Henry Wilhelm, see note 10, p. 4.
36. Henry Wilhelm, see note 10, p. 286.
37. Henry Wilhelm, see note 10, p. 3.
38. Borge Andersen, Borge B. Andersen & Assoc., interview with the author, January 1998.
39. Mark Roosa and Robert Vosper Fellow, International Federation of Library Associations and Institutions, "Care, Handling, and Storage of Photographs - Information Leaflet, "February 1992.
40. Anita Young Hallman, see note 9, p. 112-113.

### Album Slipcovers

If your album does not have a slipcase and you want to store it on an open shelf, store it in a slipcover. For most albums, a clean cotton pillowcase will serve this purpose. If you want something that looks a little more attractive, you can make a slipcover. Choose all cotton fabric and wash it well. Use a cut open paper sack to create a pattern. Lay the album on the sack and trace the outline of the cover with a pencil. To allow for a hem on the open side, extend the shape by one inch on the side that corresponds to the spine. Then enlarge the entire shape by 1/2" to create a square or rectangle just a little bigger than your album. Use this pattern to cut two pieces of fabric. Measure the width of your album's spine. Then start at the spine and run the tape measure along the top edge of the cover, down the side edge, and then back along the bottom edge until you reach the spine. Draw a rectangle as wide as the spine and the length of all the edges combined. Add one inch to each end and then draw lines 1/2" outside your rectangle to create a pattern piece that allows for seams. Match the edges of the long piece to the edges of one cover piece and pin them in place. Sew the seam and repeat with the second cover piece. Finish the cover by hemming the open edges. You can sew lace on that edge if you want a fancier look. Carefully slip your album inside, being careful not to let the page corners catch on the cover.

## Top Tips Chapter 3

- Keep all your keepsakes clean, cool, and dry and store them in a dark place.
- Avoid using acidic and chemically active substances in your albums.
- For important photos and other valuable items, mount them with reversable methods only.
- Use permanent, non-reactive inks for recording important information.
- Use paper that is acid-free, lignin-free, color-fast, and has a good finish. As much as possible, choose non-recycled papers for your albums.
- Choose safe plastics such as uncoated polypropylene, polyethylene, and the polyesters Mylar D and Mellinex #516. Avoid PVC and all vinyl.
- Use stable adhesives that have passed the P.A.T. test and limit the number of adhesives you use on a page.
- Pigment based inks, especially black, and laser copies will last a long time. Choose them for recording important information.
- Select albums with quality construction and acid-free pages with page protectors. Evaluate whether or not you require completely acid-free construction. You may make one choice for some albums and another for others.
- Provide a slipcase or slipcover for dust protection or store your albums in a closet or cabinet.
- Use acid-free storage materials for photos and supplies, especially for long-term storage.
- Deacidify or photocopy on acid-free paper any newspaper clippings or other acidic paper items for inclusion in your scrapbooks.
- Use a soft pencil to write on the back of photos on their edge. If you require a pen, use the Pilot Photographic Marker.
- Evaluate the potential effect on your photos of any decoration methods you want to use, including cropping. Do not crop self-contained Polaroids.
- Store your albums away from pollutants, wood, and humidity. Use silica gel canisters if your area is very humid.
- Store your negatives in photo-safe plastic or paper enclosures.
- Make any copies of a photo that you will need before placing it in an album. Take advantage of print-to-print, laser, and digital copy options.
- Choose good film processing and long-lasting papers. Know your lab.
- Clean, repair, and encapsulate important documents as needed.

# CHAPTER 4

# Social Scene

## ∂ Who and What You May Meet Along Your Way

For many people, interaction with a group of like-minded scrapbook enthusiasts in one of the best benefits of this hobby. Even if the group at a workshop is very diverse, they are brought together by their love of scrapbooking. For most of this chapter, I will use feminine nouns and pronouns. In my experience of my local area and the on-line scrapbooking community, the overwhelmingly majority of scrapbookers are female. I estimate I have made over 100 visits to various scrapbooking stores, most of those to two or three stores near my home. I have seen fewer than a dozen men in the stores during all those visits put together. The small entrepreneurs in this new industry are also primarily women. During the dozens of phone calls I made during my research, I spoke to only three men. Many workshop participants joke about their husbands being bewildered by their fascination with this activity. The evening scrapbook gatherings have a distinct "Girls' Night Out" atmosphere. This is not to discourage those males who are interested in scrapbooking. It is just to explain that my use of words reflects my experience in this area.

## Workshops

Workshops, or crops, are gatherings of scrapbookers in a home or store to work together on their albums using their own supplies. Though participants provide their own paper, adhesives, and other materials, they use the tools of the consultant or store sponsoring the event. This is a great opportunity to try scissors, punches, circle cutters, and sometimes even scrapbook computer programs. For tools you only want to use occasionally, workshops offer the opportunity to make what you want with those things without buying them. Another benefit of these gatherings is the opportunity to buy materials as you need them while you work. The paper, stickers, and die-cut shapes are all available to choose as you go. In some stores, a die-cut machine and dies may be available for you to use as well. A scrapbooking teacher is available to give ideas and help with techniques. Many stores offer classes in addition to the workshops. The classes focus on a particular topic or tool. A teacher instructs the participants in lettering techniques, rubber stamp usage for scrapbooks, or some other skill.

Thousands of women sell Creative Memories products and many set up a miniature scrapbook store for their customers. They buy tools, including expensive deckle-edge paper cutters and heavy-duty corner rounders, and keep an inventory of stickers, paper, and die-cuts. To allow them to teach their customers new skills, they share ideas through the network of Creative Memories consultants. The consultants offer crops in their own homes, homes of class coordinators, and occasionally at a large getaway or gathering in some other location. Creative Memories created National Scrapbook Day (the first Saturday in May) to celebrate scrapbooking and provide a chance for participants to share ideas on a grand scale. In 1996, over 2000 people gathered in a hall in Denver to work on their albums. In addition to Creative Memories consultants, and representatives of Life and Times and other small direct sales companies, some independent business women sell supplies and offer in-home workshops.

## Getaways

Jennia Hart, owner of The Scrapbooking Idea Network (www.scrapbooking.com) created a unique opportunity for scrapbookers to gather in a special setting. In 1997, she hosted the first scrapbooking cruise. Jennia had a vision of creating "a 'fantasy' workshop where any tool you could imagine was available." She also wanted an opportunity to share the ideas and techniques she had learned with participants. The event was an overwhelming success. The women had a great time and learned a lot.

For those planning to attend a getaway, on land or sea, Jennia suggests preparing ahead. "Organize your photos in advance and pre-select the papers, stickers, templates, etc. that you think you will use." By grouping your materials into sets by pages, you will be ready to actually create your layouts and get a lot done. Consider what your goals are for the event you will attend. Do you want to finish a lot of pages? Is sharing ideas or visiting with other scrapbookers important to you?

Some participants get a few pages done, but that is not their main focus. Jennia says, "To be honest, I never attend an event with the expectation that I will work on my books. I always like to spend my time checking out other people's ideas. . . you can work on your books at home, but you can't see these people's ideas at home. Getting fresh ideas might be a better way to spend your time than doing a few pages." Jennia noted that some cruise participants did complete many pages during the event. She suggests bringing a camera and lots of film to photograph layouts that appeal to you. If possible, take pictures in natural light with no flash. (A scrapbooking cruise, however, may be one of the few gatherings where this is very practical!) Since most of these gatherings are indoors, you will probably have to work with that lighting. Shoot from a slight angle, off to one side, so your flash does not bounce back toward the camera. This may prevent a glare on the photo. Using no flash and a fast speed film may also work. Experiment by photographing a few of your own pages in different lighting conditions. Then you will know how to get good results when you take photos of layouts at the event.

If you think about what you want to get from your experience, and plan for it, you will probably have a great time. Before you choose an event to attend, be sure it is organized to suit your needs. Many scrapbooking conventions are primarily a showcase for memory albums and supplies. If you want to see the newest products, they are a great option. Decide if it is important to you to learn new things at the event. Find out what is included with your registration cost and what classes require an additional fee. Be sure the classes cover topics that interest you and are at your level of expertise. Many conventions have a long cropping workshop, or space to work on albums, available. Plan ahead to take advantage of those opportunities if you want to create pages while you are there. These crops also provide an opportunity to visit with scrapbookers from around the country. To find out about conventions, getaways, and cruises, check *Creating Keepsakes* and *Memory Makers* magazines. These Web pages also list current scrapbooking events:

> www.scrapbooking.com
> www.gracefulbee.com/events/index.html
> jangle.com/shows.htm
> www.netprojections.com/scrapnet/scrapnet.htm
>   (Then go to "events.")
> disc.server.com/WebApps/calendar-add.cgi?unique=3538241

# Cyber-Scrappers

One way to get some new ideas and interact with other scrapbooking fans in your home is by visiting Jennia's site and other scrapbooking sites such as those listed in Chapter 13. On-line chats, bulletin board systems, and e-mail loops offer chances to get to know and learn from members of the on-line scrapbooking community. Details about these resources are also in Chapter 13.

My experience with these women has been overwhelmingly positive. They express appreciation for new ideas and answers to their questions and take a lot of time to help new scrapbookers as well as veterans. They give suggestions, offer moral support, and lend a sympathetic ear. While I was writing this book, almost everyone I asked for help on-line sent thoughtful, useful replies to my requests. Before visiting the scrapbooking sites, I read a lot of articles that urged people to be very cautious about interactions on-line. Though I have found that scrapbookers can be rude, that is rarely the case. I asked Myndee Reed, owner of Scrapnet (www.netprojections.com/scrapnet/scrapnet.htm), if she had any cautions for those new to on-line scrapbooking resources. She replied that she had experienced no problems. "I really believe the scrappers of the web are some of the greatest people on earth!!"

## Top Tips Chapter 4

- Take advantage of the rich resources available from interacting with other scrapbookers.
- Prepare ahead for crops and getaways by assembling only the supplies you will need for the pages you plan to do at the event.
- Make the most of the tools available to you. Plan to work on layouts that require punches, scissors, cutters, or templates that you don't have at home.
- Consider your goals for the experience and choose an event that will meet your desires.
- If one of your goals is to collect layout ideas, bring a camera and plenty of film to photograph layouts you like.
- Use natural light when taking pictures of album pages, or shoot from off to one side to reduce glare.
- Find out about scheduled scrapbooking events by reading magazines or checking out event pages on scrapbook Web sites.
- Explore the resources for sharing ideas on-line at scrapbook Web sites from Chapter 13.

# CHAPTER 5

# *Stoppers*

## 🐦*"I don't have the time, money, or talent to do this!"*

If you have been looking through some scrapbooking magazines, or at the albums of a friend who has been creating scrapbooks for years, you may feel overwhelmed. Just thinking about your own shoe boxes filled with photos stored in no particular order may make the prospect of creating a scrapbook seem daunting. This chapter offers you some options which will make the process less intimidating. If you want a collection of albums filled with your photos, written comments, and memorabilia, make it your priority to create one and work with the time and money you have.

It is important to keep this project in perspective. It is easy to become very absorbed in this activity. People frequently use words like "addict," "fanatic," and "obsessed" when referring to dedicated scrapbook enthusiasts. Check out the names of the Internet scrapbooking sites in Chapter 13. You may encounter scrapbookers who stage photo shoots to create the photos for a particular layout they want. If you attend workshops, you will meet a few avid scrapbook-makers who spend hundreds of dollars a year on their hobby but the role of family historian is most rewarding when you keep scrapbooking in perspective.

The most important question is, what are your goals for your family albums? If you visualize your finished project with these goals in mind, you will find the time, money, and resources you need. You may not have every supply and tool you want, but you will have the rewards of a family history recorded in attractive, long-lasting albums. As you read this book, look at other people's albums, and read magazines. Keep your own style, goals, and opinions foremost in your mind. When you look at the lists of events to photograph and other options for album content in the Starting Out chapter, ask yourself which memories you want to capture in your albums. Make sure your books are *yours* and not just an effort to keep up with someone else's choices or some imagined ideal. If you don't enjoy your scrapbooking time, stop and decide what you need to change. Stick to your budget, consider your family members and other responsibilities, and begin. If this is important to you, and you give it your time and energy, you will be delighted with your results.

## Time

One great challenge in life is to make time for what is most important. Making your family history work a priority is the key to getting your albums done. This means scheduling time for this activity and eliminating other activities that are not as rewarding. Time spent watching TV, surfing the Internet, or reading magazines might be cut back in order to make time for scrapbooks. Your photos will sit quietly, right where they are, unless you do something with them. They won't call out for attention. Some of the most important activities in our lives require us to set our priorities, take initiative, and work one step at a time.

Another key to using your scrapbooking time well is to stay caught up. Here, "caught up" is relative to when you started scrapbooking. Most people find it most satisfying to begin with current photos, work on the backlog as they can, and keep up with new photos as they are taken. That means filing photos and memorabilia as soon as you get them. Organize your tools and keep them in order. If possible, set goals to get all photos into albums within a year of when they were taken. Some scrapbookers like to have some perspective on events before designing the layouts to record them. The one-year time limit allows for this but will keep you from feeling like you are always playing catch up. Listed below are some specific strategies for good time usage while scrapbooking.

## Scheduling and Motivation

- Set specific goals for completing pages or set an amount of time to spend on the project each month.
- Work your way.
  - Get up early or stay up late.
  - Work for hours or in short spurts.
  - Crop alone or with others.
- If you like to scrapbook with other people, consider workshops and even scrapbooking getaways.
- Schedule time to meet with other scrapbookers if need be, to make sure you take the time.
- Plan ahead for workshops.
  - Organize all the items for several pages or spreads.
  - Pre-crop photos if that fits your page design style.
  - Decide which tools you need to take and get organized.
  - If you are on a tight budget, you may want to spend the whole time using the tools you don't have. Mount photos and add written comments later at home.
  - Always consider what tools will be available, so you can plan to do layouts that require the ones you don't have.
- If competition motivates you, participate in challenges with local friends or over the Internet.
- Use small segments of time and otherwise wasted time (travel time as a passenger, waiting time, even TV viewing).
  - Sort or crop photos.
  - Mentally plan layouts.
  - Do some journaling.
- Consider using some large chunks of time (vacations, long weekends.)
- If you like to work alone, make an appointment to work on your albums.
- Make it a habit to write daily. Even writing a sentence on a calendar or planner will make it much easier to write about important events on your pages.

## Attitude

- Be realistic and remember that small steps gradually realize your ideal.

☙ Remember, it's acceptable to keep the design simple for your pages.

☙ Progress is slow when you first learn something new. You will get faster.

## Organization and Tools

☙ Organize your material well.

☙ Put each item back where it belongs after each use.

☙ Arrange items by frequency of use. Put those favorite tools in easy reach.

☙ Use the short cuts from Chapter 7 to include more journal information.

☙ Use tools that speed up the process, such as paper cutters and trimmers, the circle cutter, computer designs, and easy to use adhesives, such as a tape runner.

☙ Trace template shapes on the backs of photos using a light box, makeshift light box, or a set of two identical templates taped or stapled together. To use the template set up, slide your photo between the two templates. Align the photo behind the shape while looking at the front. Carefully turn the templates over and trace the shape on the back. You then have no marks to wipe off the front.

☙ Work on one theme for a while. Do successive years of birthdays, holi - days, vacations or other recurring events. Even if your finished albums will go in chronological order, this approach can make it is easy to accomplish a lot in little time. If you work on your albums away from home, you can easily bring all the supplies with you to finish many pages with the same theme.

☙ If time is an issue, but money is not, decide whether or not you would like to hire someone to complete some of your albums. Many scrapbook ers would never consider this, because it is so important to them to express their own thoughts through each page but it is an option.

## Money

Creating beautiful and clever album pages does not have to be expensive. With careful planning and close attention, a family historian can take ten rolls of pictures per year, complete an album every two years, and spend less annually than the cost of an expensive dinner and movie for two. Even if you create very elaborate albums, scrapbooking is inexpensive compared to hobbies such as golf, boating, woodworking, and recreational shopping.

The most important guideline in order to stick to your budget is to buy only what you will use. Hundreds of pairs of fancy scissors sit unused in boxes and drawers across the country. Many scrapbookers have stickers, paper, and die-cuts that will never find their way into albums. A few instances of "buyers' remorse" are inevitable when you begin, but a little restraint will keep them to a minimum.

Pay attention to how the expense of small scrapbooking supplies, such as stickers, adds up. An album with stickers on every page will cost quite a bit to create. Stickers, patterned paper, stationery, and purchased die-cuts are the most expensive supplies available.

One of the best ways to limit your expenses is to share them with oth- ers. Form a scrapbooking club to use many tools, idea books, and other non-consumable resources like clip art while buying only a small amount. Here are guidelines for forming and running a club:

❧ Make these decisions at the beginning -
- What is the number limit for members?
  Six to fifteen works best to keep the size manageable and still have enough people to have a lot of tools.
- Will there be dues?
- If so, how will they be used?
- What are the group's goals?
  Sharing ideas, hosting speakers, and finishing pages are some possibilities.
- How often will you meet?
- Will you meet in members' homes?
- Are refreshments part of the plans?
- Who is allowed to come?
  Most groups find a "no children allowed" rule works well, but members with infants and small children may want to set up another arrangement. Hiring someone to help with the children may work for some groups.

Plan how you will share tools and supplies. Meet and make a list of the supplies you would like to add to the group's resources. Then have members choose which items from the list they would particularly like to own. Individual members buy and keep their tools. The person who really wants a circle cutter buys one, while another member subscribes to a magazine, or shares her clip art books. Each person brings all their tools each time the group meets. Then, if a member leaves, there may be a gap in the tools available, but it won't cause too much of a problem. Members also can buy in bulk, swap unwanted supplies, and share handouts. Some groups use dues to cover the cost of making copies of information the group wants to share. This is also an economical way to plan a scrapbooking getaway. The group can rent a vacation apartment or other accommodations, bring everyone's tools, and have a well-equipped scrapbooking marathon.

## Money Saving Tips

### Buy Smart

- Look for bargains on frequent expenses such as film processing.
- Delay gratification: avoid costly one-hour film service and wait for sales.
- Try tools at a store or a consultant-sponsored workshop before you buy.
- If you can't try before you buy, purchase only one of any particular tool, such as a fancy template, until you know you will use that type of design aid.
- Consider how often you will use a stamp, punch, scissors, or template.
- Don't buy tools you know you will use only a few times. Use them at workshops or borrow them from a friend.
- Stamps are an economical choice only if you will use them frequently and decrease your use of other items such as stickers.
- If you use designs only once or twice, clip art is cheaper than stamps.
- Plan purchases so you can take advantage of sales and coupons.
- If you live near a craft superstore, watch for 30% and 40% off coupons.
- Put off all major tool purchases (paper cutters, pen sets, heat embossing tools) until coupon time.

- Compare prices and shop around.
- Shop on-line businesses and watch for their sales.
- Consider your shipping and handling costs when shopping by mail.
- Watch for free and low-cost shipping; you can save as much with these deals as with sales.
- Buy in bulk at office supply stores, but only if you will use or trade it all.

## Use Everything

- Use the outlines:
  Mount sticker letter outlines with pattern paper behind them.
  Use die-cut outlines as:
    1) templates to trace the shape on the page or piece of paper.
    2) frames for photos or journaling.
    3) stencils to use with pigment ink on a sponge.
- Cut designs out of rubber stamp and scrapbooking magazines and catalogs (if the paper is acid-free) and use them like a sticker or clip art to decorate a page.
- Use your paper scraps for punched shapes, to cut shapes with a die-cut machine, and for small mats on your pages.
- Look for unused art tools around the house such as children's stencils and rulers with cut-out shapes to trace.
- Search through old catalogs, newsletters, and other potential sources of clip art. One of the best sources I found was a university's quarterly continuing education bulletin.

## Don't Buy

- Swap with others, especially if you have a stockpile of unused supplies.
- Swaps are seldom economical unless you can swap for exactly what you need. On-line secret pal swaps are a lot of fun, but don't usually save you any money.
- Ask for scrapbooking supplies for gifts. Circulate your wish list.
- Coordinate a class with a direct sales company representative to earn free supplies and gifts.
- Use free storage containers, such as film canisters for punched shapes or craft knife blades, and sturdy baby wipes containers for scissors, stamp pads, rulers, and long handle punches.
- If you already have Internet access, get free fonts, clip art, advice and ideas on-line.

## Make Do

- Journal in pencil until you can afford the pen colors you want. Later, go over the penciled information with ink.
- Be sure all photo-mounting you do is reversible. If you want to create more elaborate pages when you can afford more supplies, you can redo a few later.
- Cover mistakes with stickers, paper, an opaque marker, or a doodle with a pen.
- Use up the supplies you have before you buy more.
- With a craft knife, cut shapes out of plastic from lids, plastic pizza trays, and other objects to make templates.

- Cut stencil plastic with decorative scissors to make fancy rulers.
- Use cookie cutters as patterns to cut out shapes.

Consider whether or not a do-it-yourself tool is a significant money-saver. Templates and fancy rulers are cheap enough that it is usually worth the small cost to purchase these tools designed for the task at hand.

## Talent

You have the money and are willing to make time for this. What holds you back is art anxiety and scissor fear. If you do not consider yourself to be artistically inclined, creating scrapbook pages like those in magazines can seem impossible. The best cure for these ailments is to just do it. Start with photos that are not your favorites, or with a set of duplicate prints, so any "beginners' blunders" do no real damage. Work through the design projects in Chapter 7 and watch your fears be replaced with satisfaction and maybe even a little pride. You can do this, and the more you do it the better you will get.

This book will help you avoid potential pitfalls with hints about how to use scrapbooking tools well from the start. You will also learn how to add that little something a page needs to be complete. Chapter 9 shows you how to overcome mistakes and other possible problems. Stop comparing what you think you can do to the ability of others. Your design skill will improve, but from your very first page, you are creating a priceless keepsake that will be treasured by your family. They will see your effort and love, not your crooked letters.

While I researched this book, I came across a lot of top-notch helpful advice to scrapbook makers. Mixed in with that good information were a few myths. These myths scare and discourage people before they start and need to be debunked.

### Erroneous Rules

⏵ Myth: You should write a lot on your pages or they are incomplete.

Writing on your pages is fun. (Try it; you'll like it.) But it is not required. If you don't write much at first, consider leaving space that will permit adding more journal information later should you decide you want it.

⏵ Myth: You should do all your journaling by hand. That it is written in your own handwriting is as important as what you say.

That is really on a handout I received. It is nice to include your own handwriting in your books. Your children will appreciate it (especially if it is legible). Include a handwritten compiler's note at the end of each album if you like. Do your journaling by hand, with computer printouts, with sticker letters or any other way you like. You might write more if you copy the samples from a lettering book and get comfortable writing on your pages. *The ABC's of Creative Lettering* is great for beginners and experienced scrapbookers.

⏵ Myth: Make sure someone takes pictures of you too, because your children are entitled to a complete record of their childhoods.

That one came off of a handout too. The first part is good advice. You'll probably be glad you have photos of yourself at 30 or 40 when you are 80.

The second part is a guilt-producing myth. No one is entitled to scrapbooks or even photo albums. Food, shelter, clothes, and education maybe, but not scrapbooks. These albums are most meaningful when the creator loves the process. If you choose to do albums for your children, make sure the real reason you make them is because you want to do it.

🐾 Myth: You should get your albums completed and then stay caught up.

See the answer to the previous myth. If you want to stay current, make it a priority and do it. If you want to work leisurely for years and years, or stop and then go back to it, that is fine. If you create any albums at all, they will give you and other people enjoyment.

🐾 Myth: Work only with duplicate photos and store the rest in a photo-safe box.

Duplicate photos are great. It is usually a good idea to get them if you are doing albums for your children or other relatives. It is nice to have duplicates to work with when you first begin, so you have back up photos available should you accidentally decapitate someone in a photo. Once you get some experience, it is usually wasteful to make sure a full set of photos is stored somewhere other than in your albums. Make sure your negatives are stored properly. For very special photos, storing a copy may be a good precaution, but it does not make sense to do that with your whole collection. If you were given the belongings of one of your ancestors, which would you be more likely to keep: a box of photos or a set of well made albums?

🐾 Myth: The photos should dominate the page.

Only if you want them to. Choose what you want to stand out on the page. Learn to notice what makes a design element draw the eye, so a large yellow die-cut that is unimportant to you won't accidentally overwhelm your photos. If you want a piece of clip art or a sticker to draw the viewer's attention, that is fine. It's your album.

🐾 Myth: Make sure your scrapbooking doesn't take any time away from your family duties.

What do you do just for you? If this is rewarding and fun, take the time to do it. You deserve it. Delegate some work if need be to make time for this.

🐾 Myth: Use only archival, totally photo-safe materials in your albums.

Make informed choices and consider how each material will effect your photographs and hold up over time. Then you decide. You may choose one level of preservation standards for some albums and another level for others. Sometimes you may even make exceptions to your own rules.

🐾 Myth: You should start with your most recent photos and work back.

Yes, I gave that advice earlier in this chapter, but not as a "should." For many people this method works best to start. It is not, however, a rule. If you want to make a heritage album with all your older photos for your first project, read Chapter 3 and then do it.

🐾 Myth: There are rules for making good scrapbooks.

Nope, there aren't. There are guidelines, there are recommendations, and there are methods that work well for most people. There are no rules. Your albums are yours, and you should have the final say in fashioning them. Use the resource of this book and others listed at the back. Write, stamp, trace and experiment on separate pieces of cardstock and then mount them on your page to reduce anxiety over making a mistake. Relax and enjoy; you may do this even better with experience, but you can't do it wrong now.

## Top Tips Chapter 5

- Keep scrapbooking in perspective and keep your own goals for your albums in mind.
- Make it a priority to create your scrapbooks and schedule time to do so.
- Work your own way: with others or alone, early in the day or late at night.
- Plan ahead for workshops and get organized before you go.
- Use small segments of time to do tasks like cropping photos and journaling.
- Write in a planner or calendar daily to make it easy to write information in your albums.
- Be patient and work step-by-step to complete your books.
- Choose simple designs for some pages.
- Organize your supplies and tools and put things back after each use.
- Use tools that speed up the process such as circle cutters, trimmers, and tape runners.
- Use a light table to trace shapes on the back of your photos before cropping or attach two identical templates together and trace.
- Work on pages with one theme for a while.
- Set a budget and stick to it.
- Pay attention to the cost of little items like stickers. They add up quickly.
- To save money, limit the amount of expensive supplies (stickers, stationery, pattern paper) you use.
- Consider shipping and handling charges when looking for mail-order bargins.
- Wait for sales and coupon deals, especially to buy expensive tools.
- Use everything: die-cut outlines, sticker letter outlines, paper scraps, and art tools you already have, such as children's art rulers.
- Swap for what you need and buy in bulk (if you will use it all).
- Use up what you have before you buy more.
- Don't accept the myths. Educate yourself and then make the choices you think are best when creating your scrapbooks.

# PART II

# Creating Albums

# CHAPTER 6

# Starting Out

## 🔊 *How to Organize and Begin*

Family historians have three major categories to organize: photographs and other keepsakes to mount in albums, scrapbooking supplies and tools, and notes and layout ideas. Put all three sets of materials in a system to keep them organized. You will enjoy your scrapbooking time much more and be more productive if you do. Organized supplies and environments foster organized thoughts. You will have an easier time creating pages that please you, if you can find all your supplies. This also keeps you from buying duplicate pairs of scissors or pens. It helps you take advantage of sales, because you know what you have and what you need.

Before working on these three areas in-depth, complete the following checklist. These suggestions will prevent you from losing or missing out on information you need, damaging photos with poor storage practices, and spending too much money.

## Starting Out Checklist

1) Gather all photos, documents, and memorabilia in one place. This may involve asking other people to give or lend you photographs.

2) Separate the items so that newsprint and other paper items are not touching the photographs. If time permits, immediately remove photos from damaging albums such as those with black paper or self-stick pages. If not, complete that step as soon as you can. Keep the photos in order and save the pages (store them separately from the photos) if there is any information written on them.

3) Contact elderly relatives for family history information and borrow photos or pay for duplicates.

4) Read the Top Tips for Chapter 3 (or the whole chapter).

5) Think about your completed album project. How do you want to group your photos in the albums? Are you making books for anyone other than yourself? Will you make laser copies of the finished pages for additional albums for children or grandparents?

6) Decide how much money you want to spend and make a budget for supplies. The questions and information in this book will guide you as you choose the best materials for your albums.

7) Consider your overall goals for your album collection. What do you want your books to document, and what messages do you want them to express?

# Organizing Photos and Album Memorabilia

The process is simple but usually takes time. Gather, sort, label, and copy your photos and keepsakes as needed.

## Gather

Gather from everywhere: frames, attics, boxes, old albums, friends and family members. Don't wait. People relocate and, after a while, elderly relatives forget what they have.

> ❧ Here are some records and keepsakes that will be useful:
> - photographs
> - computer files - letters, school reports, speeches
> - calendars and planners
> - tax records
> - letters with the envelopes and stamps
> - postcards
> - maps
> - school papers
> - greeting cards
> - brochures (vacation and company)
> - business papers
> - military records
> - certificates and ribbons
> - name origin certificates (Traces company sells these.)
> - anything that brings back memories
> - anything that tells your story -
>     poems, cartoons, Ann Landers advice columns
>
> (Even if all these items do not go into the albums, they will jog your memory and make journaling easier.)

Anything you think belongs in your album is appropriate to include. My father died when I was nine years old. Several years later, I read an essay in *Seventeen* magazine, written by a teenager who was also very young when her father died, and she expressed her feelings very beautifully. The essay was titled, "Daddy, I Wish I Knew You!" I copied the article and mounted it on the album page with my father's obituaries. At the end of the title, I wrote in "Better!" That page expresses my feelings so the article belongs there.

## Sort

Before you begin to sort, you need to decide how many albums you will make and if the photos will be arranged chronologically or by some other system. You do not have to determine how many actual books you will create; you just need to decide if you will compile separate albums for different family members. Your decision will help you choose which groupings to use for sorting your keepsakes. Have a separate sorting box for each album, or set of albums, you plan to create. Acid-free boxes and hanging file folders are good sorting containers. (If you use regular file folders, it is a good preservation practice to line them with an acid-free folder or to place acid-free white copy paper on each side of the folder so the photos do not rest against acidic paper.)

Divide the photos by:

1) family member
    2) type of photos
       size
       styles
       black and white
         3) benchmark events - W.W.II  - or -   categories
            4) life seasons
              5) decades
                6) years
                   7) months

If you sort by categories, each set will be comprised of photos with common themes: holidays, military service, vacations, etc.,

## Label

Briefly record key information about each photo or group of photos. Many times it is best to do only a little labeling, at this point, so you can finish quickly. If details come to mind that you are afraid you will forget, be sure to jot them down.  Otherwise, do most of your writing when you create your pages. If you are going to write directly on the photos, write on the edge and use a soft pencil, a wax pencil like Stabilo, or a Pilot Photographic Marker. You may also make notes on acid-free slips of paper and place them beside the photos in the box or file. Self-stick notes have an adhesive that can leave a residue on your photos after you remove them. Avoid using them directly on photos, especially on the front.

## Copy

This step refers to copying photos and memorabilia, and especially acidic newspaper clippings. If your photographs and negatives are stored together as you start this process, order the reprints you need for the albums you have planned. You may also need to copy photos lent to you. If you are going to have copy negatives made for special photos, do it before you put the original print in an album. Also, copy original photos you won't place in your albums, so the copies will be available to include. Other family members may want copies and might share the cost with you.

- Copy photographs and have negatives made as needed.
- Photocopy newspaper clippings and other acidic documents that reproduce well on a black and white copy machine.
- Choose how to include oversized and three-dimensional items.
  - Take a photograph of the item, perhaps with the owner.
  - Have a laser color copy made and reduce it if need be.
  - Place it in a keepsake box.

## Hints to make the gather, sort, label, copy process easier:

- Work quickly when you are sorting. Save the reminiscing for when you do the pages.
- Color-code by album projects or people to improve your filing system.

- If you can, find a place for this project where you can leave it out. Then you can work on it for a minute here and there as you have time.
- Recruit other family members to help you.
- Be realistic. Enjoy your progress and take the time you need.
- If you are using the page protectors sealed on three sides, you can place all the photos, paper memorabilia, and decorating items for one page into the protector and store it all together. When you are ready to start making pages, all the items will be in one place. This method can scratch the plastic though, so avoid handling the filled page protectors very much before completing the page.
- Remember to store your negatives separately from your photos.

## Choice of Albums

There are four general styles of albums available that offer photo-safe materials and pages that will hold photos, written information, and page decorations. The types are listed below with their potential advantages and disadvantages. Remember that your best choice may be to use more than one kind of album in completing your set of books.

### ❧ Three-Ring Binders

These albums come in at least two sizes, 8.5"x11" and 12"x12". The pages slip inside a plastic sheet protector and the protectors are held in place with the rings. The "D" ring type usually puts less stress on the pages than the "O" ring design.

**Pros**
- The 8.5" x 11" size uses standard size pages that are widely available.
- The page size is the same as a regular-sized laser copy.
- Pages are easy to move around as long as two sheets of cardstock (one for each page) are used in each sheet protector.
- Slipcases are frequently available for dust protection and added support.

**Cons**
- The rings are visible between the pages when the album is viewed.
- If the album is dropped, the rings can pop open and the pages fall out.
- Smaller pages give less room for journaling and require using fewer photos.
- Extra dust protection, available in the form of a slipcase or slipcover, is recommended if you use standard top-loading page protectors.

### ❧ Spiral Self-Contained Albums

These albums have paper pages with heavy card covers and a metal spiral binding.

**Pros**
- Covers can be personalized easily.
- The pages lie flat for viewing.
- These are frequently economical.

**Cons**
- Page protectors are not available for this type of album.
- The pages tear easily with rough handling.
- The order of the pages is set and cannot be changed.

## ❧ Strap-Bound Expandable Album

This design binds pages or page protectors into an expandable album with flexible straps. If the pages are bound in, page protectors are available to slip over the pages from the side. For albums with the page protectors bound in with straps, the pages slip in to the top of the protector.

### Pro

- These are commonly available in 8"x10", 12"x12", and 12"X15" sizes.
- The pages lie flat with no space between them when the album is open.
- Many designs of prepared pages are available, including lined, wedding, baby album, and border decorated pages.
- Some of these albums come with good quality guarantees.

### Cons

- With the page bound albums, pages are designed for placing photos on both sides. This makes it impossible to add a page in between those two pages.
- All pages are white unless you mount other paper over the entire page.
- Slipcases are not widely available for this style.
- The pages of some of these albums have edges made from acidic paper.
- The larger page sizes are more expensive to laser copy.
- Most laser printers' maximum copy size is 11"x17", so 12"x12" pages are cropped when they are copied.
- With the page bound type, you can't photocopy or print from your computer directly onto the page.

## ❧ Post Bound Expandable Album

These albums come in at least two sizes: 8.5"x11" and 12"x12". The pages slip inside a plastic sheet protector and the protectors are held in place with posts. In some of these albums, the pages and protectors are bound in with the posts.

### Pros

- The 8.5" x 11" size uses standard size pages that are widely available.
- That page size is the same as a regular-sized laser copy.
- Pages are easy to move around as long as two sheets of cardstock (one for each page) are used in each sheet protector.
- There is no gap between the pages when the album is open.

### Cons

- The posts can put too much stress on the pages or page protectors.
- The smaller pages give less room for journaling and require using fewer photos.
- Extra dust protection is recommended if you use standard top-loading page protectors. If a slipcase is not available, use a slipcover or store the album in a cabinet.
- The pages usually do not lie completely flat when the album is open.

If you can, visit a scrapbook store or look through some catalogs to see what these types of albums are like. Then consider your options as you decide how you want to organize your photos and memorabilia.

## Album Organization Options

Organize and group your photos into categories and sequences that appeal to you. If you want your albums to tell your story in chronological order, the organization system described in the previous section, Organizing Photos, provides you with a system to use, but it is not your only option. Many scrapbookers find that system too confining and prefer to work in themes or by events. A wedding album is an example of a one-event album; Christmas, Hanukkah, and Kwanza albums are recurring-event albums. Theme albums are organized around themes such as friends, hobbies, military service, or school experiences.

Ask yourself these questions when you plan your album organization:

1) For how many people will you create albums?
2) Will any of the albums be laser-copied to provide additional books?
3) Do you want to organize in chronological order?
4) Would you prefer to work primarily in themes?
5) Are you working with others on your scrapbooks (your children, adult siblings, parents, or professionals)?

Some professional scrapbookers create albums for other people. If you will be working with one of these professionals, consider that in your plans. If your children are creating their own albums, set up guidelines concerning which of your supplies and photos they may use. Beyond that, give young people a lot of freedom to create their scrapbooks their way. Sometimes parents are tempted to give a lot of directions, because they want their children's albums to look a certain way. If this is true for you, you may enjoy making one set of albums for your children and letting them do separate albums themselves with duplicate prints. Listed below are album categories to review as you set up your own system.

- **Chronological family albums**
- **Child's album**
- **Wedding album**
- **Vacation album**
- **Holiday album**
- **Military album**
- **Church service or Peace Corp. album**
- **New home album**
- **Farewell or Commemorative book for a retiree**
- **Gratitude book**
- **Business album** - Record of a company's history/an individual's career
- **Heritage album** - Photos and records of your ancestors
- **Collective extended family book** - One album is maintained (family members may rotate this job) and pages are copied and distributed at reunions.
- **Friends and Family album** - Sections for each family that regularly sends you photos
- **Portraits album** - Contains only professional portrait photos
- **Anniversary album** - Goals, dreams, and other annual remembrances

I first heard about the last three categories on the list from Brenda Birrel, owner of Pebbles in My Pocket. The Friends and Family album is a lovely way to organize photo holiday cards, school photos sent by relatives, and any photographs you have of special friends and family. In my own albums, if I was present when the pictures were taken, the photos of my extended family and friends are usually placed in my chronological family albums. The photographs they send me, taken when I wasn't there, go in my Friends and Family album. I have a section for each family that sends pictures regularly. Occasionally I will put photos I took in this book to finish up a page or to make sure I have a good picture of everyone in a family.

The Portraits album is a special scrapbook that contains only professional portraits that are usually oversized prints. Avoid cropping these photos. Use cut-out frames over them for enhancement. If you prefer, and if you usually order multiple prints from portrait sittings, mount some portraits in your chronological album and others in a separate book. In one of her catalogs, Brenda describes how much she enjoys watching her "children grow up before my eyes" as she thumbs through that one special Portrait album.

A special type of album can organize your photos to use as a teaching tool or personalized storybook. All children enjoy these books, but home-schooling families may want to make a collection of these as part of school time. If you do that, create the scrapbooks *with* the children, not just *for* them.

- **My own story book** - Copy a children's story book using photos of your child to illustrate the story.
- **ABC album** - Put the letters of the alphabet on the pages, one or two letters per page, using pens, stickers, die-cut letters, or even clip art. Place photos of objects beginning with each letter of the alphabet on the pages.
- **123 album** - A number book with photos, stickers, or other page decorations used for the objects to illustrate each number. For fun, include a 100 page.
- **History book** - Combine heritage photos and narratives with historical information about the times in which your ancestors lived.

## Heritage Albums

Unless you happen to have all the photos of your ancestors that exist, and all the personal information you want, you will need to approach gathering these treasures systematically. Organizing this project is overwhelming to many people, so here is one step-by-step process that works well.

1) If you are married and are compiling photos for you and your spouse, start four boxes or files: your mother's side, your father's side, your spouse's mother's side, and your spouse's father's side. On the outside of the file or box, place a sheet of paper for two lists: general contents of the box and a log of letters you send and receive.

2) Write down all you know (or think you know) about each of those four family branches. Put that information and all the pictures, certificates, clippings, etc., that you already have into the appropriate box or file.

3) Look over your "family trees" and scan for any potentially helpful older relatives. I don't mean to be macabre, but put a star by the oldest ones

and any that are ill and make it a point to talk to them soon. Ask these special people for information you want for your album, but use this project as an opportunity to express your appreciation and love for them as well.

4) Write a few SHORT letters, starting with letters to the relatives with stars. Ask for specific information: "Aunt Lu, do you have a list of all your brothers and sisters and their birthdays (and would you please include information on Uncle Unmentionable, just so I will have a complete list)?" Unless you are very close to the relative, be sure to send a self-addressed stamped envelope along too. If they call you, take careful notes, including who told you what information.

5) When someone answers your letter, send them a thank you note. Use some stickers you decided you didn't want to use in your albums, or some other decorations, to personalize the letter.

6) File their letter in the right box.

7) In a separate letter from the thank you note, send another short letter of inquiry if you think that relative may have more facts you need.

8) Once you get going, this project takes on a life of its own. I suggest you schedule a set amount of time each week or month to continue the project, but don't allow the research to run your life.

9) When you have a lull in writing and answering letters, go through and fill in the pieces of the puzzle. Even if you do this on a small scale, consider entering all your information into a computer using a program such as Family Tree Maker. The most basic version will work for you if you don't plan to immerse yourself in genealogy research. If you want to do in-depth family research, talk with a genealogist (an avid amateur would work) or explore this hobby on-line. My favorite site for beginners is Treasure Maps. If you want more information, explore this amazing road map to thousands of genealogy sites: Cyndi's Genealogy Links (www.oz.net/~cyndihow/sites.htm). An alternative is to get some genealogy forms to fill in to organize your information.

10) Plan your heritage albums. I strongly suggest you consider using an album with slip-out pages. I was sure I had all the available photos of my ancestors before I compiled an album. Then my aunt obtained wonderful photos of my grandfather's family from a distant relative. Because my photos were mounted on both sides of my pages, I had to figure out how to fit in the new photos in without disrupting the sequence. I was able to arrange the pages in a way I like, but the new pages interrupted three carefully designed two-page spreads.

11) If you do choose moveable pages, you may still want to wait until you've gathered a lot of information so you don't need to redo a page of the same grandfather two or three times. If you know you have most of what is available for one family line, start there if you're anxious to get an album started.

12) If you find reluctant relatives try this:
    a) Offer to give them a copy of the finished product. With written information, this is not difficult to do, especially if you have entered it in a computer.

b) Respect what they don't want to discuss and focus on what they want their grandchildren to remember about the family.

c) Use a snippet from one relative to get another one talking: "Aunt Janie said blah blah blah." Many folks can't resist correcting or adding to someone else's story if they can.

d) Keep good notes and write down where you got everything so you can compare it to public records, information from other relatives, and published records such as those on the Internet. If you suspect some information is incorrect, write that down.

e) If you are trying to get a copy of a photo, offer to get a negative made and send them back the original and an extra copy. It will only cost you a few cents more to get two copies and then you will have a valuable negative. If they won't let the photo out of their sight, take them and the photo to a place that makes a print-to-print copy while you wait. You could also get a color photocopy or scan the photo.

## Which Albums for Which Scrapbooks?

As you decide how to organize your collection of scrapbooks, consider which albums will work best for which books in your set. Review the Top Tips in Chapter 3. Decide what level of photo-safety you want for each album. You may decide to make one album using strict standards of conservation materials. These are the guidelines for an archival album:

### Archival Album

1) Use a well-made completely acid-free album that has a slipcase, or store the album inside a cabinet.

2) Make sure the page protectors are made from uncoated polypropylene or the photo-safe Mylar or Mellinex polyesters.

3) Choose page materials and papers that are completely acid-free, lignin-free, color-fast and not recycled.

4) Use tested photo-safe pigment inks, and use only black for important information. Laser prints may also be used.

5) Separate materials: photographs and paper memorabilia stored on separate pages, in separate page protectors. Clean, repair, deacidify, and encapsulate important documents, or photocopy them.

6) Use only adhesives that have passed the P.A.T. and do not use them directly on the photographs. Use corners, slits, or slip-in frames.

7) Choose high-quality photo finishing from a lab that uses Fuji paper, or other photographic papers, that fared well in accelerated aging tests. Have the pictures printed leaving a white border around the edges.

8) If it is practical, store the photos or the album pages themselves digitally on a CD-ROM as well.

If you want more freedom to use a lot of design materials or a certain style of album, make sure the following guidelines are met to ensure lasting results.

## Photo-Safe Album

1) Use an album made with photo-safe materials such as buckram and cloth. Make sure that any part of the album that touches your pages is made of acid-free, inert materials. Avoid PVC and vinyl of any kind. If the album will be handled by children, make sure it is structurally strong. Provide some kind of dust protection for the album.

2) Use page protectors made from uncoated polypropylene or the photo-safe Mylar or Mellinex polyesters.

3) Choose page materials and papers that are completely acid-free and lignin-free. If you live in a humid environment, check colored paper for color-fastness before using it to mount fiber-based prints.

4) Use tested photo-safe, permanent pigment inks to record information. Laser prints may also be used. For decoration, chose pens, colored pencils, watercolors, and chalks that are chemically stable. Use ink-jet printouts only for decoration, not journaling.

5) Deacidify paper documents and mount them so they do not touch the photos on the page. If you photocopy them on to acid-free paper they may touch photos.

6) Use only adhesives that have passed the P.A.T. Use corners, slits, or slip-in frames for valuable fiber-based photos.

Because I love many of the stickers, die-cuts, stationery, and colored papers available, I use those in most of my albums. I am selective about manufacturers and I follow the second set of guidelines above. I do, however, keep in mind that many design materials have unknown longevity. I don't know how those stickers will look, or how true the paper colors will stay, fifty years from now. I remember that as I design a page. If a sticker falls off, can I add another one, or a punched shape, to refresh my page years from now? This is a minor concern in my opinion, but one worth considering.

Because I treasure the photographs and biographical information I have of my ancestors, I am in the process of creating one album that meets all the top archival criteria above. It takes a little more effort, because fewer decorating supplies meet those strict standards, but it is very interesting. The look is completely different from that of my other albums, and I find it very appealing. This album contains copies of photos of my ancestors. The modern copies should last longer than the originals; that is why I use them in this book. Above all, this album is made to last. I will add photos to it every few years, being very selective and including only a few special favorites. For me, creating one archival album is a way to have my cake and eat it too.

### Tips

These tips conclude the section on organization of your photographs and memorabilia to place in your albums:

- If you would like to make a bound baby book more durable so you can comfortably allow a young child to handle it, insert the pages into page protectors and place them in a three-ring binder album. Carefully use a craft knife to cut the pages out along the edge of the spine of the book.

- Instead of sending duplicate photos to grandparents, send them color laser copies of album pages. Begin by giving them an album with a few pages in it and then send more, already slipped into page protectors, for birthdays and holidays.
- Think ahead before you order portrait photos. Consider what prints you need for your albums, children's albums, gifts, and pictures to frame. With mass-market portrait chains in particular, obtaining reprints after your initial order can be very difficult. Because these photos are copyrighted works, you cannot legally obtain more photos without the permission of the photographer. Remember, the photos on display will fade much faster, because of exposure to light, than those in your albums. If you want to hang your favorites on the wall, consider getting two copies so one is preserved in an album.
- Here are some ways to use your duplicate and extra photographs:
  1. Collect for ABC books.
  2. Punch shapes or cut letters from them.
  3. Frame them.
  4. Use them for photo crafts such as mounting them on boxes.
  5. For photos taken from too much of a distance, filled with tiny people, punch out the faces and use them for a border.

## Organizing Your Supplies

My suggestions for supplies to buy first, and ones to add as you develop your scrapbooking style and decide what methods you like best, are listed below. If an item is marked with an asterisk (*), experiment with it first at a workshop or a friend's house. These are items some people find they don't like, or find that they prefer one style as opposed to others. I love my big Boston pivoting blade paper cutter and prefer to use only that style. Other people love the rotary blade type, especially if they have young children at home or want to cut fancy edges. The blade on this type of cutter is interchangeable with wavy and other decorative blades. Since the blade is rolled, rather than being lifted up, children are less likely to injure themselves on this model.

### Must Have
pages
page protectors
adhesives/corners
Stabilo pencil/soft graphite pencil
good black pen with photo-safe, permanent ink
ruler
oval template
good scissors
pH pen
organizing supplies
   zipper-seal bags, folders, shoe boxes -something for dust protection
(Acid-free storage materials are best, but short-term storage in acidic boxes is acceptable if that is all you have to use.)

### To Add Later
album
dust protection for album: slipcase, slipcover, or closed cabinet storage

various colors of cardstock and paper
Pilot photographic marker
pens in two or three colors
circle templates/circle cutter
decorative ruler/border template*
corner rounder
short blade scissors
personal trimmer with a pivoting or sliding blade*
  or a paper cutter with a pivoting blade or rotary blades*
deckle edge scissors
lettering book such as the *ABC's of Creative Lettering*
instructive design books such as *Core Composition, Punch Happy,* and
  *Drawing With Young People*
clip art books or computer collections
light box or a substitute: a glass table-top, a piece of Plexiglas over a table
  opened out to take a leaf, or a sunny window
red eye pen and magnifying glass*
small stickers for accents, if you plan to use stickers
organizing supplies
  good negative storage supplies
  silica gel canisters for storage if your area is humid
  binders & pages, folders, file boxes to store stickers and die-
  cut shapes and paper

## Luxuries, But Nice To Have

colored pencils
more pens
scrapbook font software such as Lettering Delights by Inspire Graphics or
  D.J. Inkers Fontastic
regular fonts from software or the Internet
other basic shapes templates
more rulers/border templates
stencils
quilter's quarter-inch disk
basic shape punches such as heart and star
decorative corner rounders/punches
hand-held punches such as the micro dot and tear drop
more scissors*
craft/mat knife
cutting mat
metal edge ruler
compass and swivel knife (holds pens too)
seam roller or bone folder
almost all consumables
  various colors of cardstock and paper
  patterned paper
  stationery including imprintables that give a nice frame effect
  die-cut shapes
  stickers
  ribbon in natural fiber or with known chemical and acid content

organization and planning supplies
    cardstock swatch book, made or bought
    magazines, idea books, and newsletters such as:
        *Familyphoto, Creating Keepsakes, Memory Makers,*
        International Scrapbook Association newsletter
    totes - Crop-In-Style, Cropper Hopper, other totes
    pen organizer
    Piece Keepers and Highsmith storage supplies
    tool case, tackle box, literature holder, business files: rolling,
    drawer; use a laser printer cover for dust protection
    archival boxes for long-term storage

## Extras/ Special Interest

spot pens or photo oils for hand tinting*
rubber stamps
pigment ink pads
embossing powder
heat tool to set inks and embossing powders
brayer
embossing stencils and stylus
art air gun*
crimper
scherenschnitte scissors
papercutting patterns*
templates with various shapes
more punches
stencil burner to make your own stencils*
prepared pages
specialty books such as *Picture Pie, To Our Children's Children, Castle of the Pearl, Punch Your Art Out, The Pop-Up Book, Joy of Photography, Snowflakes Made Easy,* and *Scrapbooker's Best Friend*
calligraphy book
deacidification spray
document tape
polyester sheets for encapsulation
double-sided archival tape

## For Pros

deckle edge paper trimmer or Fiskars rotary paper trimmer
heavy-duty corner rounder
oval cutter/oval mat cutter
Phantom Line special tracing tool that casts an image from copy to page
computer and scrapbook/genealogy programs
scanner
die-cut machine and dies
(If you are going to make this major investment for a store, use these strategies to make the most of it. Scout out stores in your area to see what dies are already available. If you will be the first store with a machine, buy a set of letter dies. Consult with stores in other areas to find out the most popular shapes. Consider ordering the geometric shapes to use for the designs in the *Picture Pie* books.)

## Supply and Idea Organization Tips

1) Consider your needs for home storage and portable storage if you attend crops or workshops.
2) Establish a place for all your supplies and return them there after use.
3) Write your initials with a permanent marker on tools you take to crops.
4) Make a note of where you purchased paper and stickers so you can easily get more.
5) Use catalogs to organize your buying plans.
6) Mark the outside of your picture envelopes with a highlighter, if you do your processing at a store where you find your own photos when you pick them up.
7) Keep your planner open and near you during the day to jot down experiences, layout ideas, and other plans for your albums.
8) Once a day, or at least once a week, jot notes about your life and your family's experiences on a calendar or in a planner. This makes journaling much easier, especially if much time passes by before you create the pages for those times.

## Supplies Storage

Frequently, you can purchase great storage containers for scrapbook supplies in the sports, office supply, or home repair departments of discount stores. Rubbermaid makes a tool case designed to hold a drill that is the perfect size to store 12" x 12" paper and pages. My main organizer is a generic plastic box that opens on two sides and has many compartments.

Although products made specifically for memory album makers are usually great for storing your supplies, they can be expensive. Weigh your financial considerations, your desire for an organizer with compartments tailored to your supplies, and how you use your storage. Do you work at home, attend many of workshops, or both? If you work on your pages away from home, you will need something for portable storage. Many scrapbookers use whatever bag they have at home, but those who purchase special cases are very happy with them. Pockets and loops are made to fit your tools and materials, and at least one model, the Crop-In-Style bag, takes up very little space because it stands upright. If possible plan at-home and portable storage at the same time so you create a system that works for both needs with no duplication.

### Stationery, Stickers and Die-Cuts

In addition to storage for punches, adhesives, and other tools, you will need a system for storing and organizing:

1) stickers
2) stationery and patterned paper
3) die cuts
4) decorative photo corners
5) art clipped from acid-free paper such as advertisements

Some scrapbookers store these items in file folders, small index card boxes, CD holders and even coupon organizers. If you would like to keep together all those supplies with a similar theme, consider this system.

Fill three-ring notebooks with pages in these sizes:
1) regular 8 1/2" x 11" page protectors
2) 4-pocket pages for photos
3) baseball card holder pages with nine pockets
4) APS pages for long narrow prints

The paper goes in regular protectors and stickers usually go in the baseball card pages. The die-cuts and large stickers fit into the 4-pocket pages and border stickers are stored in the APS pages. Some people also use regular size protectors and sew in the divisions they want. Carefully cut openings for the pockets by slipping a piece of cardboard in the long pocket and then making the cut, if you sew the pages. Because this system uses top-loading protectors, it works best for home storage. If the binders are not toted around, the items are less likely to slip out the top of the pages. Zipper-seal plastic storage bags can also be used to store supplies in three-ring binders.

With this system, all the birthday paper, stickers, die-cuts, and miscellaneous art is all together within a few pages. This organization makes it easy to file ideas with your supplies. If you see a cute idea for a way to use a certain sticker, jot it on a self-stick note and place it on the pocket where you store that sticker. You will want to devise your own category system, if you use this method. It is handy to keep a list of your categories at the front your binder. Here are my categories to give you an idea of a list:

- Sayings
- Ballerina
- Birthdays & Celebrations
- Baby
- Animals
- Charms, vehicles, toys
- Letters, dots, bows
- Graduation
- School
- Christmas
- Angels
- Red patterns, Mary Engelbreit
- Warm and masculine patterns
- Business papers
- Easter and church
- Halloween
- Kites, pals, and dolls
- Travel, transportation
- US maps, mime, train
- Outdoors, west, vacation
- Gardening
- Houses
- Plants & Fall
- Floral, Victorian, wedding
- Hearts and Valentines
- Seaside & swimming
- Trees, mountains, countryside
- Earth, weather, sky
- Fantasy, castle

## Clip Art

If you use a lot of clip art, you may want to organize it in categories as well. Since the subject matter available is different for clip art than it is for the supplies mentioned previously, I have a separate category list for clip art. The letters are the codes I write on the back of the pages upon which I mount the clip art.

- Borders - B
- Travel - T
- Misc. - M
- Sports - Sp
- Performing Arts - PA
- Graphic Arts - GA
- Fantasy - F
- Outer Space - OSp
- Outdoor Activity - O
- Animals - A

- Nature - N
- Nature Plants - NP
- Nature Mountains -NM
- Holiday-New Years, Valentine's- HN
- Holiday-Easter - HE
- Holiday-Patriotic - HP
- Holiday-Halloween - HH
- Holiday-Thanksgiving - HT
- Holiday-Winter/Christmas - HWC
- Women - W
- Reading - R
- Girls - G
- Grandpa - Gr
- Couple - C
- Family - Fam
- Babies - Ba
- Children - Ch
- Birthday - BD
- School - S
- Buildings - Bld

It is convenient to work with clip art using this process.
1) Photocopy the image from your original.
2) Clip the image from the copied page and apply a temporary adhesive to the back.
3) Mount the image (or images) on a piece of white acid-free paper.
4) If you want to copy the design you have created onto cardstock to use as a page, make the copy and the page is ready for you to use in your layout. If you will be clipping the final image to add to a page, you may want to copy several pieces of art onto the cardstock. Save the others to use on other pages in the future.
5) Make a good copy of the design you made to be filed for future use. The piece of clip art can be moved before you use it next time, in case you want to place it in a different spot on the page.
6) File your copied design pages and the removable clip art pages in the appropriate category for future use. Write the code on the back and give the new page a number. For example, if you already have 10 pages of "babies" clip art and you add one, you will write "Ba-11" on the back of this page. This allows you to file it easily the next time you use it. The numbering is only necessary if you have a large collection and want to keep it in a special order.

## Storage Specifics

### Templates
Punch holes in templates and file them in three-ring binders. You may also store them in an expandable file or file folder. With a permanent marking pen, label each template on the edge that will be at top of the file or outer edge of the binder. If the template edges catch on each other, place a sheet of paper between them.

### Pens
Be sure you store your pens horizontally. This keeps the tip moist and in good condition. Options for pen storage are pen organizers such as Markers in Motion, silverware drawer organizers for just a few pens, or a homemade pen organizer. A clever idea from Barbara Wilkes uses cans with cardboard dividers. Each divider is the width of the can and is folded in half. When you insert them in the can, they look like pie wedges. The cans sit upright for use and can be placed in a box for horizontal storage.

### Rubber Stamps
Clean, unused pizza boxes are an economical option for storing rubber stamps. Because the acidic paper of the box can weaken the rubber, line

the boxes with acid-free paper. Stamp the design of each stamp in the place you want to keep it and they are well-organized and protected from dust.

## Punches
Craft organizers with several tiny compartments are nice for storing punches and even the punched pieces of paper.

## Rulers
Silverware drawer organizers hold fancy rulers and long, thin stencils. The shorter drawer organizers work well for storing embossing stencils.

## Scissors
For working at home, a bulletin board with push-pins creates a handy organizer to hang scissors and templates within view and make them easy to reach.

## Oversized pages
To protect 12"x12" pages and organize photos and decorations to use on the page, use 2-gallon zipper-seal plastic bags.

## Paper
To store paper, line regular file folders with white acid-free copy paper to protect the cardstock from acid migration.

# Planning Materials, Layout Ideas and Note Storage
## Tool Reminder

To ensure you do not buy scissors you already have, and to make it easier to see what tools and paper are available while you design pages, create a supply and tool reminder. On one 8 1/2" x 11" piece of white cardstock, mount a small square punched from each color of cardstock you have in the middle of the page to make a small color wheel. This first step is only necessary if you are a picky color fanatic (like I am). From the same sheet, punch out a shape with each one of your punches, and trim a small bit off the edge with each of your paper edgers. On the back, with the pens themselves, write the name and color of each pen. Slip the page in a sheet protector and take it with you when you shop for supplies. If you carry a day planner, you may prefer recording the supplies you have, including pasting in punched shapes, in a section of your planner.

Because I love color so much, I also have two metal rings filled with pieces of cardstock. Each time I find a new color, I trim a 1" x 3" strip, punch a hole in it, and add it to a ring. These rings are available in several sizes at office supply stores. Some suppliers, such as Paper Cuts and Pebbles in My Pocket, sell these swatch books. These are so helpful when buying paper and when choosing colored paper as you work on a page. Usually, with this tool handy, you won't pull out quite so many pieces of paper just to put them away again when you find they don't match your photos. Yes, I do label each one with the store where I bought it, a number, and the name of the color.

### Magazines and Idea Books

A great way to store scrapbooking magazines is in three-ring binders using long plastic magazine holders, which are available at office supply stores and come in packages of 12. Slip the magazine through the slit, and the punched plastic sticks out the back. Then you place them in binders. This also works with thin idea books. Some companies sell scrapbook papers bound in booklet form. The booklet covers have layout ideas, so I put all the covers I have together in one magazine holder and keep them in a binder.

Place photocopies of magazine indexes at the front of the appropriate binder for easy access. These same binders can be used to store your other lists, class handouts, and miscellaneous album ideas.

### Planning Notes

❧ Lists for scrapbook planning:
- Price comparisons
- Items to buy when they go on sale
- Goals for albums
  messages you want to convey: "Johnny is good at sports."
  completion: "Finish the wedding album by New Years Day".
- List of photos to take
- Events
- Feelings
- Quotations, famous and from family members
- Family sayings, "You're in the dog house!"
- Songs, song titles
- Questions to ask of yourself or others
- Page ideas, design ideas
- Items to copy (regular copies or laser color copies)
  art work, medals, patches, quilt sections, tassels, special fabric, wedding gown lace, pressed flowers, cover of a favorite book, items you really like that are printed on acid paper suchas: greeting cards, wrapping paper, maps, brochures, sheet music of special songs, recipes, tax returns, business or marriage licenses

### Page Order Planner

If you are completing an album that has pages in a set order (spiral bound, for example) or pages in which both sides are used to mount photos, set up a page order planner. Write out a planning sheet that lists the subjects of the photos that will go on each page, in the order in which they will go. If you plan it out, you can work on any page you like as long as you count back to where it belongs in the sequence.

### Planning Photos

Be spontaneous as you record your life and the lives of your loved ones with your camera. Keep it handy and watch for moments you want to capture. The lists below are not "to do" lists. They are suggestions to help you to remember to grab that camera at times you might not think to do but later will be very glad you did.

## Pictures I'm Glad I Took

Job Day - household chores and the movie reward at the end of the day
blowing bubbles
water fights
bugs
children's rooms
pregnant
children with each of their relatives
first apartment
before-during-after: remodeling
talents (juggling, putting both feet behind his head)
work place
each room of my childhood home

## Pictures I Wish I Had

doll collection before I sold it
first car
children with each best friend
first job
Vietnamese refugee family
getting ready for special events
before-during-after: exercise program

## Subjects to Finish a Roll of Film

pets
home inventory
hobbies & collections
heirlooms
quilts
gifts
jewelry
crafts and artwork

## Annual or Periodic Photos

a day in the life: follow child throughout a typical day, taking photos
family in front of the house
children on the first day of school
    holding a sign with their names, name of school, and date
local annual events - the same part of town each year
baby with the same stuffed animal
    take photos monthly the first year, and then once or twice a year

If they are important to you, don't put off your planned shots too long. My town has an annual parade each summer to commemorate the arrival of the pioneers who settled this area. Through 1996, the day before the parade hundreds of people would set up lawn chairs along the sidewalk of Main Street to reserve themselves a place. I wanted to go at about five o'clock in the morning and take a picture of this scene. For me it perfectly captures the quiet, safe quality of my town. I finally made plans to take the picture in 1997. That was the year the police put up signs forbidding people to leave chairs out overnight!

## Top Tips Chapter 6

- Work through the Starting Out Checklist on page 51.
- Gather, sort, label, and copy your photos and keepsakes before placing them into albums.
- Consider the advantages and disadvantages of each album style before buying. The best choice may be to use more than one kind of album in creating your collection.
- Review the options for organizing photos in your albums and choose the system you will use. Pages 56 and 57 list some choices for album groupings.
- Make a plan for collecting family photos and information if you want to create a Heritage album. A plan is provided on pages 57-59.
- Choose what level of preservation standards you want to use for each of your albums. Feel free to use different standards for separate albums.
- Send grandparents laser copy album pages instead of loose photos.
- Consider your long-term needs so you order enough prints after a portrait sitting. Reprints can be difficult to get with portrait chains.
- Choose tools judiciously and don't buy more than you need to start.
- Add more tools as you discover your style.
- Plan for at-home and portable storage if you attend workshops regularly.
- Set up a system to organize tools and supplies and put things back.
- Binders and pocket pages can store stickers, stationery, pattern paper, and die-cuts together by themes.
- To get the most use from your clip-art, set up a file system for easy access.
- Store pens horizontally to preserve their tip in good condition.
- If you have a lot of tools and are buying more, create a tool reminder.
- Store magazines, idea books, and notes in three-ring binders.
- Keep a "photos to take" list. Use it to finish up a roll of film.

# CHAPTER 7

# Style

## Snazzy Scrapbook Design

Once you have gathered the photos and memorabilia for a scrapbook page, it is time to make some design decisions. This section will guide you in selecting an art style and offer some general design guidelines. The following sections will take you through the design principles and elements experientially. Explore the styles you want to use in your scrapbooks and work through the layout lessons. When you finish this process, you will find that page design is really quite simple and can express your personality in your albums.

If you have looked through some scrapbook idea books or magazines, you may have noticed that most of the layouts have a very contemporary style. Some have cute lettering and design touches such as clip art or stickers. For current photographs, especially of children, these cute and modern styles work well. For some scrapbookers, however, confining themselves to these types of page decor feels limiting. Some find that those styles don't reflect their personalities and that they would like another approach. In this chapter, nine distinctive scrapbooking styles are described and illustrated. Most decorating supplies that are available fall into one of these nine categories, more or less. Some stickers or stationery combine two or more styles. These divisions are not meant to put scrapbook art into nine boxes; they are intended to assist you in finding design approaches you like and encourage you to consider using a variety of styles in your albums.

## Design Principles

Before reviewing the style categories, consider a few basic design principles to use as you create your pages. Perhaps the most important suggestion in this chapter is to do your page layouts in two-page sets, or spreads. A spread is any two pages in your scrapbook that are next to each other when the book is opened. Even if they contain photos of completely separate events, it is a good design principle to make sure they coordinate. The colors, balance of elements, and styles of the two pages will be seen together. For example, avoid placing a soft infant portrait with pastel colors across from a red and green Christmas scene.

In addition to considering adjacent pages, briefly consider the entire album and its intended audience. The albums I create for my teenage sons have a very different feel than the ones I create for myself. Some pages are almost identical, but some are very different. I use a lot of Victorian clip art on the pages of my albums that feature my sons as infants, but the baby picture pages in their books have a more contemporary touch. Choose your style with the album owner in mind. If you are beginning a scrapbook for a friend or relative, ask them to look through some pages of other scrapbooks or scrapbooking magazines with you. Ask the person which pages they like and which ones they don't like and why. You can also show them the style examples in this chapter and note their preferences.

Remember that you can include more than one style in a single scrapbook. For some albums with a single specific focus, like a wedding album or a commemorative album, you may choose to use only one style throughout the book. For others, such as a chronological family album, including several styles will be more appropriate. Usually it is best to use one style, or a hybrid of two related styles, for each spread.

The last general design consideration is choosing the focus of a layout spread. The specifics of emphasizing page elements are covered later in this chapter. For now, just consider what you want your viewer to notice when they look at a page or a spread. What is most important to you or the album owner? The focus may be one photo, or two or three. It may be the written information or a telegram. This focus should help communicate the primary message you want this layout to send.

- We were a wild and crazy bunch in high school.
- This child has brought us more joy than we ever could have imagined.
- She was a talented, take-charge woman ahead of her time.
- We had a blast that day!

As reflected in these examples, sometimes the desired message is simple and immediately obvious when you look at your photos. Sometimes it must be considered for a while in order for you decide which idea you want to express and then how to communicate it clearly. If you keep in mind which item you want to be the focal point of your page, the messages of your scrapbooks won't be overshadowed by the design and decoration.

## Design Styles

In addition to cute and contemporary, you have many choices of decorative styles to enhance your pages. I have chosen nine groupings based on the stickers, papers, clip art, and design tools available. Some items fit cleanly in one category, others are a blend of two, and a few designs really don't go with any of the styles described. In the following pages you will find descriptions and illustrations of each style, along with lists of products that generally fit each category. As you read about the styles, consider the overall feel that each is likely to create. Will the effect be cute, clever, beautiful, charming, striking, soothing, or exciting? Are some styles mutually exclusive? Could you have a Floral and Lace layout that is also Rustic? Notice which styles appeal to you and which do not.

### Floral and Lace

Flowers, lace, and fabric-look papers characterize this style. Many sticker companies feature flowers in their product lines and floral paper is abundant. In addition to these products, this style can be created with a variety of scrapbooking tools. Punch art flowers are easy to create, and stencils and templates frequently feature flowers and lacy patterns. Most decorative scissors, except pointed ones like pinking shears, coordinate with the Floral and Lace style. Many corner punches contain flower shapes or give a lacy look to the paper. Use hand-held punches and decorative scissors to create a paper lace look. Hot Off The Press and other companies offer papers that look like lace or fabrics such as satin. This style can use all colors, if they are carefully coordinated. Look at flowers to learn which colors work well together. Whether it be the complementary violet and yellow of a pansy, or the softer monochromatic blend of two yellows in a daffodil, flowers know color.

## Whimsical

A Diane Hook design is used to illustrate the Whimsical style. All of her D.J. Inkers characters have a distinctive appeal. This style is definitely cute and popular with many scrapbookers. A distinctive feature of Whimsical art is the presence of a definite personality. Diane's creations, as well as the critters in many Mrs. Grossman's stickers, have character. The expressions on their faces and the little touches in their clothing give this feeling of whimsy. The D.J. Inkers company offers this thought, "our mission is to create a smile with what we do." That effect, together with the presence of characters, defines the Whimsical style. This style frequently overlaps with the Country Charm category. The pen-stitching, gingham, hearts, and stars in D.J. Inkers' designs make them a blend of Whimsical and Country Charm. Several D.O.T.S. character stamps, Provo Craft people and animals, and Lucy Rigg's bears are other examples of the Whimsical/Country Charm style blend. Suzy's Zoo animals, some Sandylion characters, and Bryce and Madeline stickers from Melissa Neufeld have a Contemporary/Whimsical look. Punch art animal faces and some die-cuts, such as the Ellison jester, can add whimsy to your pages. Scalloped and wavy scissors accentuate whimsical design elements on a page.

## Country Charm

Hearts, gingham, polka dots, and items depicted in a primitive art fashion characterize the Country Charm style. Pen-stitched and dotted accents, as well as a round, puffy look also are featured in Country Charm art. Provo Craft, D.O.T.S., Peddler's Pack, Main Street Press, and many R.A. Lang designs feature this style. Gingham, dotted, and other fabric-look patterned papers work well with this style. Many of Northern Spy's pattern papers (with their hand-drawn look) reflect the Country Charm Style. This look is easy to create with pens and cutting tools. Some punches, such as rounded hearts, rounded stars, pigs, and cows have a definite Country Charm look, as do some templates, especially those from Provo Craft. Scalloped, pinking, and other simple scissors coordinate with this style. Country Charm colors are muted. For example, soft green, dark evergreen, and soft peach colors work well together in this look.

## Victorian

The Gifted Line company has been largely responsible for a resurgence in the popularity of this style for scrapbook art. They sought out and reproduced genuine Victorian designs on their stickers and cards. The Victorian look is distinctive and easy to identify. Detailed and delicate renditions of turn-of-the-century subjects are the identifying feature. Gibson Girl illustrations, and illustrations in many other Dover Publications clip art books, are other examples of this style. Many of the spot illustrations in this book are Victorian designs from Dover books. Laser-cut photo corners sometimes have this look, as do many corner punches. Hand-held punches used to create a border design coordinate well with Victorian art. Many fancy rulers and scissors that feature curves with points create a Victorian look.

## Art Nouveau

This style was very popular at the beginning of the twentieth century. It features flowing, bold lines, symmetry, and sometimes floral themes. Although there are not many scrapbook products that specifically reflect this style, it is very beautiful and versatile. Dover Publications offers many Art Nouveau books, including some beautiful color works by Alphonse Mucha, with lovely designs. In addition to this clip art, laser-cut corners, corner punches, and some die-cut flowers create this look.

## Nature/Rustic

Outdoor scenes, muted or neutral colors, and nature elements create the Nature/Rustic style. Usually the objects from nature are depicted realistically or in a slightly stylized fashion in this category. If it's cute, it probably isn't rustic. Geopapers offers many designs that fit this category as do some RA Lang and Melissa Neufeld products. The Paper Company, Sonburn, and Frances Meyer have many stationery designs with a Nature/Rustic look. Some pattern papers in warm, muted colors and dark greens and blues reflect this style as well. Die-cut shapes such as trees, mountains, and camping equipment convey this look. Decorative paper edgers that have a jagged design, as well as deckle scissors, work in this style.

## Modern Art

This look is very clean and has a bold feel to it. Modern Art frequently features geometric shapes and bold design elements. It is more representational than realistic. Shapes and lines, rather than specific identifiable objects, are prominent. The Modern Art look requires less supplies than most other styles. Colored paper, simple shape templates, scissors, and pens can give this look quite easily. Geometric shape stickers, such as those from Mrs. Grossman's and Frances Meyer, can be used in this style. Paper House has several sticker designs that fit well with Modern Art pages. The geometric shapes available in punches, die-cuts, and templates are also useful here. Because crisp lines are a part of this look, paper cutters and circle cutters are helpful. Wide-tipped pens can also add appropriate accents.

## Contemporary

This category can include many types of designs. Generally, Contemporary features a modern look that is distinctive in its simplicity or realism such as the photo-look stickers from Paper House. Most of Mrs. Grossman's stickers reflect the Contemporary style, as do most Frances Meyer and Stickopotomus stickers. Clear colors and simple lines characterize stylized Contemporary art. Many crisp, bright stationery designs and patterned papers fit this style. Most of the punches, die-cuts, and templates available can be used on Contemporary pages. The popular collage photo arrangement, with pictures tipped at angles to each other, is Contemporary, as is the cropping technique of silhouetting a photograph (or cutting around the people and removing the background).

## Fantasy

This category is characterized by characters and objects that are imaginary. Fairies, mythical beasts, and super heroes are all Fantasy design elements. Many clip art books feature Fantasy designs, as do some Sandylion Stickers and stationery. Some designs, such as the Disney characters, are both Fantasy and Whimsical. Generally, if "cute" is my first thought when I see a design, I consider it Whimsical. Fantasy pages can use soft colors or bold colors depending on the nature of the characters used. Fairies call for different colors than do super heroes.

Some scrapbook art does not fit in any of the nine categories. Ethnic designs such as Celtic, East Indian, and various African and Native American motifs are other specific styles. The work of some artists, such as Mary Engelbreit, is hard to categorize. Even though I do not consider her work to fit cleanly into one of these categories, it can be used as the basis of a unified page design. The color choices, clean lines, and presence of particular patterns such as checkerboards are distinctive. These elements can be carried through in finished page designs that feature Mary Engelbreit stickers or paper. Even though they do not include all possible page styles, the categories are a creative tool. Use them to choose expressive elements that fit your personality, to create variety in your albums, and to design harmonious pages with elements that work well together.

Floral and Lace

Whimsical

Country Charm

Victorian

Art Nouveau

Nature/Rustic

Modern Art

Contemporary

Fantasy

## Borders and Line

When you design a layout spread, decide whether or not you will use borders before organizing the rest of the page. Borders can go all the way around each page, all around the outer edges of the two pages, or just run across the opposite edges of the pages (top and bottom or the two outermost edges). For 8.5" x 11" pages, partial borders usually work best.

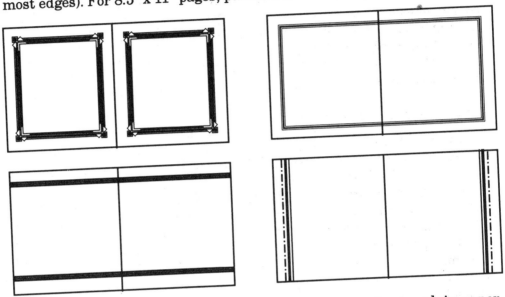

Borders can be created with clip art, punches, fancy scissors, plain paper, stationery, rulers and pens, or stickers. The border defines the rest of the space to be used and so it needs to be done, or at least planned, before the rest of the page is arranged.

To learn about borders and line, create a simple layout using these steps. Choose a set of photos you want to crop simply using just a paper trimmer or cutter and possibly a template with simple shapes such as circles or ovals. Select two or three colors of plain cardstock that coordinate with your photos. One dark color, a light muted color, and a neutral such as beige are easy to use together. Choose a fancy ruler and/or a pair of fancy scissors that fits the theme of your photos. If you confine yourself to these tools for this layout, you will learn about line.

### Line

Crop your photos and decide whether or not you will use borders. If you choose borders, plan those first. Experiment with the scissors or ruler you chose. Cut some mats from scrap paper and place them behind your photos. Doodle on some scratch paper. Use the fancy ruler or a straight ruler. Draw single and double lines, thin and thick, free-form and straight. Dot accents on the points of your line. Look at the lines in your photos. If there is a gently flowing landscape line, accentuate it with the lines you draw or cut from paper. Notice that many straight or curved lines work well, but many scalloped or jagged lines make the page look too busy. Cut a mat for one or two photos with fancy scissors and to set them off, but cut fancy mats for all the pictures and the page looks frenetic. Jagged lines have a different feel than flowing lines and thick lines present a bolder image than thin lines. Decide what the various lines communicate to you and choose accordingly. Be sure to leave space for journaling and consider this element in your design. You may create a cardstock box or two for your words or spread them around the pages.

Notice how you can use the lines on your page to lead the viewers eye. Some page elements, such a people in photos and drawings, create the illusion of a line. If a person in a photo is looking off in one direction, that draws the viewer to look that way as well. Position photos so the people look in toward the center of the page or spread. This keeps the eye moving around the layout instead of veering off the page. You can use the lines of mats, and the lines created by the arrangement of the photos, to direct the viewer's attention around the page. Use the lines in your design to focus attention toward your most important page elements.

## Borders with Rulers

If you are using fancy rulers, you may want to make some border templates. These can be cut from cardboard or plastic. They are squares or rectangles cut a little smaller than your page size. They can be finished by adding a decorative edge. I prefer to keep templates smooth and hold the rulers against them in order to add a decorative edge. If you are new to tracing decorative ruler edges, go slowly especially with any rulers with jagged or pointed edges. Start with a wavy ruler until tracing becomes easy for you. If you have the thick acrylic rulers, you can lift them off the page by taping pennies on their backs. This trick is especially useful for writing with opaque ink pens. It keeps the ink from seeping between the ruler and page and smearing.

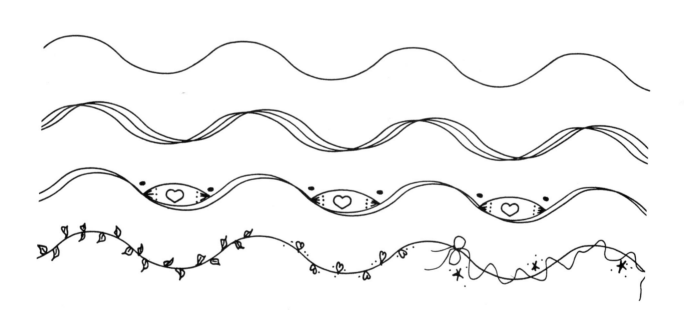

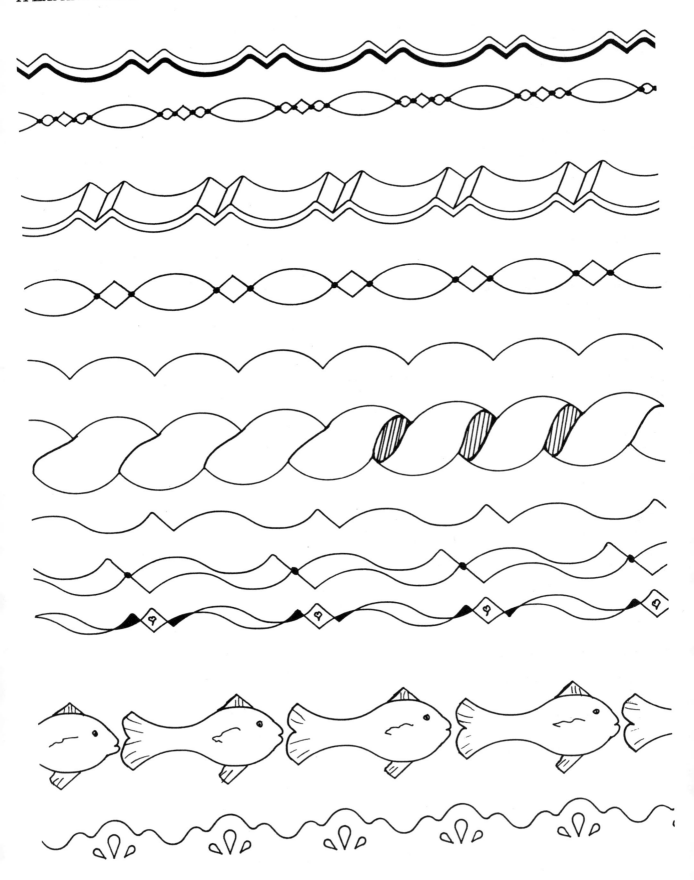

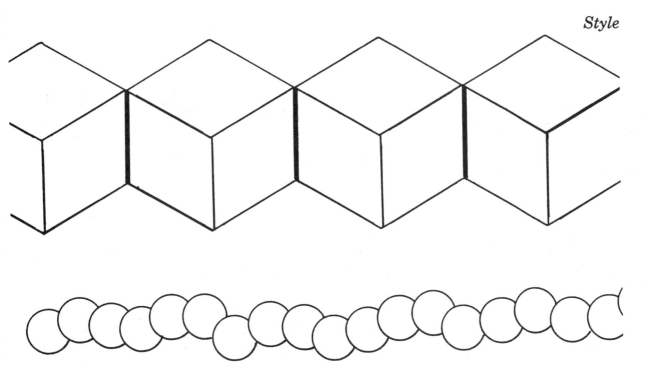

## Clip Art

For future layouts, explore the use of line with clip art. Line drawings from books, computer programs, and the Internet offer a variety of page enhancements. Clip art is available in virtually all the art styles discussed previously. It is a versatile way to add emphasis and decoration without overwhelming your photos. Unlike stickers and stationery, black line clip art is almost always a subtle accent on a page because it adds no color. If you want an illustration of this type to stand out, color it. Colored pencils or special scrapbook pens may be used for this purpose. Remember that most images printed on an ink-jet printer will smear if colored with pens. Colored pencils work on those printouts; whereas laser printed and photocopied images permit the use of pens. Another option is to trace clip art with the use of a light table (or a substitute such as a glass table with a lamp under it or a sunny window). Because of its usefulness for many scrapbook design techniques, I consider a light table or substitute an essential tool. Once you use one regularly, you will wonder how you ever did without it.

## Templates and Stencils

Another way to use line in your layouts is by tracing templates and stencils to decorate your pages with line drawings. These decoration techniques are versatile and economical. A final suggestion for exploring the use of line on your pages requires a special tool. A compass that is sold with a swivel blade craft knife can also be used with thick scrapbook pens. This can be used to create a variety of circle designs, make simple line accents to use with circle-cut photos, and to draw arc designs.

## Balance and Shape

The next element to explore is shape. Whereas lines define space and direct the eye strongly, shapes make up most of the substance of the page design. Shapes carry easily detectable optical weight. A big shape is "heavy" and a little shape is "light." This is why this layout exercise combines a focus on shape with learning the design principle of balance. When a layout is balanced, it is visually pleasing and all parts of the page are easy to view.

### Shapes

For this layout exercise, select photos that will be easy to crop into different size shapes: some that you want to crop to a small size and some that will be larger after they are cropped. Use a circle cutter or circle template, if you have these tools. In addition to the photos, choose some die-cut or traced-and-cut shapes and some small punched shapes or stickers. Again, select two or three colors of plain cardstock that coordinate with your photos. One dark color, a light muted color, and a neutral such as beige are easy to use together.

### Circle Cutter

If you use the circle cutter, follow these guidelines for the best results:

1) Be sure your blade is sharp; replace it if it gets dull or the point breaks.

2) Notice the correct cutting direction and remember to swing the blade that way.

3) With the pedestal-type circle cutter, be sure to keep a firm downward pressure on the top to hold the paper or photo in place as you cut. You do not need to apply pressure to the cutting arm and blade, however; just moving it in a circle cuts well.

4) Use glass as a cutting surface. If your cutter does not include a sheet of glass, purchase one from a glass company. This makes the cutter work so much better than it does with a cutting mat.

5) After you think the circle is cut, move the part of the picture you trimmed off. If it moves, the cut is done; if not go around again.

6) If you want to cut a smaller circle with the pedestal-type cutter, you can take the cutting arm off and slip it back on upside down. Turn the cutter over and carefully use it upside down, holding the base of the tool with your hand and resting its top end on the table.

7) Make a circle cutter template. From a sheet of mylar or stencil plastic, cut circles ranging from the smallest to the largest your cutter will make. Label the cutter settings and circles on your template with the circle size. Use this template to place over your photos and choose the best circle size before cutting. It can also be used to trace circles on your page.

8) If you are working without a template, center the circle cutter over your picture. Get down close to the cutter and swing the blade around *above* the photo. You will see the exact cut-line and can adjust the blade.

9) Practice, practice, practice! Use blurry or bad photos as well as different weights of paper. The circle cutter is very easy to use, but a little practice will give you the cleanest cuts.

10) Use your circle cutter to cut frames for Polaroid photos. Cut the outer

shape of the frame and then cut a circle from the middle. Mount the mat on the page over the Polaroid print. This hides the white border without cutting the print.

11) Use the circle cutter to economize on paper. Cut a mat for a photo to size and then use the cutter to remove the middle portion that will be hidden by the mounted picture. Use this circle for another mat, to make punched shapes, or for other page decoration.

## Punched Shapes

If you are punching shapes from paper that you plan to use on your page, such as a mat or border strip, use the punch features to line up your shapes. Many punches have notches on their central points. With a ruler, mark your paper at evenly spaced intervals and line up the notches with these marks before you punch. You can also use the back stop of the punch to space a row of shapes the same distance from the edge of the page.

## Cropping

Crop your photos into shapes of different sizes. If you do not have a light table or substitute, tape two identical templates together. Slip your photo in and position it by looking at the template on the front. Hold it steady, turn it over, and trace the shape on the back of the photo with a soft pencil. When you cut, turn the photo not the scissors. Cut into any deep corners, rather than cutting in a continuous line in and out of a tight space.

## Balance and Placement

Spread the cropped photos and other design shapes out in front of you. Begin to arrange the photos on the two pages, keeping in mind which one or two pictures you want to be the center of attention. Notice that little photos tend to look out of place near the bottom of the page and large photos usually make a page top-heavy if placed too high. This is not a rule, just a tendency that is the usual result of this type of placement. Notice that overlapped items become one larger item spatially. Explore adding and moving elements with an eye for balance and focusing attention on your key photographs. Remember to include your journaling space in your design plans. For this practice layout, make a box, circle, or other shape to contain your words so they will act as a shape for you to manipulate. Be sure you have items of many sizes to use in creating balance.

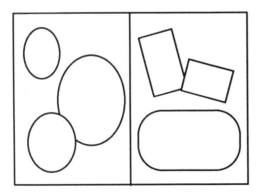 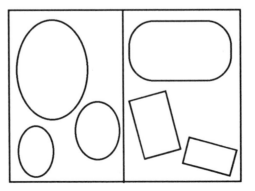

Triangular shapes (and photo arrangements) create a stable solid feeling. Circles and rectangles provide fluid and formal design influences respectively. Tracey Isidro's book, *Punch Happy*, and the *Picture Pie* books by Ed Emberley are wonderful shape primers. These books will help you discover the basic shapes hidden in all the objects in your environment. They also provide clever ideas for creating page decorations.

## Optical Weight

Notice that several small objects, like a few stickers or punched shapes, have the same optical weight as one larger object. If the balance in your layout seems just a little off, place small shapes in a couple of locations and notice the results. If you want to make an important photo even heavier, mat it. Experiment with the number of objects you use in your design. For informal balance, an odd number of objects is usually easier to arrange into a pleasing, balanced layout.

## Symmetrical and Assymetrical Balance

Formal, or symmetrical designs, give a very polished look. For pages of snapshots, however, the look is usually too stiff. Symmetry works well for a page with a single modern photo such as an 8"x10" portrait. It is also sometimes appropriate for pages with several antique portraits because these photos have a very formal look. You can use some symmetry, such as a uniform border, and still create a less formal appearance by arranging the photos asymmetrically.

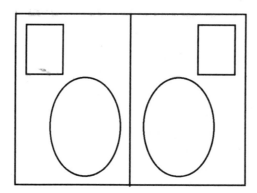 

## Finishing Touches

Look at a detailed object, such as a photo, and at a plainer shape. Notice which one has more optical weight. Consider the detail, as well as the shape and size, of an object as you evaluate its place in your design. Finally, notice that darker objects are generally heavier than lighter objects. Continue to arrange your page elements until you are pleased with your layout. Remember to look at the shapes created by open spaces. Those shapes also effect the balance of a design. When it looks good, move yourself or the pages so you can look at them upside down. If the photos are flipped, it is easier to notice the balance and overall attractiveness of the design itself (without being distracted by the content of the photos). Make any last adjustments and mount the items on the pages.

# Unity and Color

Color is one of the most enjoyable aspects of creating scrapbook pages. The variety of solid and patterned colored paper available is amazing. In this section, I encourage you to experiment with color combinations. Place different colors sided-by-side and see which ones look good together. I particularly urge you to do this with paper and your photos each time you create a layout. Remember, the main function colored papers and decorations serve is to enhance your photos and memorabilia. If you want your pictures to take center stage, choose colored papers that highlight them.

Most people are familiar with the basic complementary color pairs: red and green, blue and orange, yellow and violet. These combinations are striking and beautiful. If you have played with these colors in page design, however, you probably have found them tricky to use. The powerful contrast between these colors makes them draw the eye strongly. Remember that the brightest colors are most prominent and your photos are seldom as bright as vibrant paper. Anything else on the page, such as photographs, are overwhelmed by complementary colors in their truest, bright hues. If they are used in very small amounts, such as the thin lines of a pen-drawn border, they are much less problematic.

## Subtle Colors

Remember the entire spectrum of complementary colors, however, when you consider using them in your page designs. The red color family includes a whole range of shades and tints from deepest burgundy to dark pure red to bright true red and on through the roses to a pale "barely-there" pink. All these reds are the complements of all the greens. When you think red and green, you may immediately visualize Christmas color schemes. The color combination of pale pink, light mint green, and deep evergreen, however, creates quite a different image. Very light tints and dark shades of colors can be much easier to use in decorating album pages than their bright cousins. Muted colors that are almost neutrals, like an orange that is almost a brown, are also easier to use than bright hues.

As we scan our choices in a catalog or scrapbook store, most of us naturally are drawn to brightly colored paper. There is nothing wrong with that, or with using that paper in your albums. Consider, however, your goals. If photos, memorabilia, or original artwork are what you want telling the story on your pages, they need to capture the viewer's attention. Remember, in a few years or a few decades, your photos will fade. That high quality acid-free paper you use has color that will probably last longer than the dyes in your photos. Over time, even if the photo colors started out bright, they will fade and be overshadowed by too-bright background paper.

Am I suggesting that you trash all your bright background paper? Not at all. Here are a few suggestions for using it effectively to meet your goals for your albums. The one place that less is definitely not more on a scrapbook page is in a journal entry. Viewers appreciate the well-narrated page. Nothing, with the possible exception of the photos, is valued as highly as the words on a page. For those extra special stories, particularly on the pages with less than great photos, consider matting your handwritten or word-processed narrative on a bright color.

As I mentioned earlier, small accents of bright colors, such as punched shapes, can be used to accent and balance pages without detracting from your main focus. Consider using that bright paper as a background mat, border, or other accent for a page devoted entirely to journal information. This could be family history information, the narrative of an important event, a family tree diagram, or even a photocopy of a newspaper article. Enjoy color as you create your albums, but remember to keep in mind where you want your reader to focus.

## Color Relationships

Colors next to each other on the color wheel are analogous colors. They blend harmoniously with each other. Complementary colors are opposite one another on the wheel and create contrast when placed next to each other. Triadic colors lie in a triangle on the wheel and are energetic combinations that can be tricky to use.

| Analogous (neighbors) | Complements (opposites) | Triads (triangle) |
|---|---|---|
| red/orange | red/green | red, yellow, blue |
| yellow/orange | | |
| green/yellow | blue/orange | orange, green, violet |
| green/blue | | |
| blue/violet | yellow/violet | |
| violet/red | | |

Muted light and dark examples of warm and cool versions of the colors are listed below. Notice that it is hard to have a cool orange or a warm pale violet.

| | Warm (gold or warm red undertone) | Cool (blue or white undertone) |
|---|---|---|
| red | warm pink/brick red | cool pink/burgundy red |
| orange | peach/rust | _____ |
| yellow | gold/golden brown | ice yellow/cool brown |
| green | lt. country green/olive green | mint green/pine green |
| blue | turquoise/teal blue | ice blue/navy |
| violet | _____/plum | lavender/deep violet |
| neutrals | ivory-warm gray | cool creme-cool gray |

## Classy Color

For this practice layout, gather the set of photos you plan to use. Lay the photos out in front of you and place a piece of yellow-orange or gold paper near them or under them. Look at the skin tones of the people or the colors in a landscape. Remove that paper and place a blue-violet or ice blue paper by the photos. Shift the two papers back and forth and notice which one generally makes the photos look the best. One color may seem to wash out the photos or accentuate unattractive highlights. Once you decide which looks best, look at the Trio Chart at the end of this section. If the gold made the photos look better, warm colors will probably work well for your page. If the blue or blue-violet gave the best effect, choose cool colors.

To learn more about color, work with the coordinated colors listed in the Trio Chart. These trios enhance photos, focus attention on the page, and are aesthetically pleasing. Using these combinations, or choosing just warm or cool colors for a spread, is not required for good pages. Remember, there are no rules. These groupings, however, have been very helpful to scrapbookers seeking a more sleek and coordinated look for their pages. Some people get overwhelmed when they work with more than the six basic colors. Working with warm and cool versions of each of these colors is sometimes easier than thinking about all 12 colors on the color wheel.

Choose 2 or 3 colors from each trio (plus a coordinated neutral if desired) to use for matting, background, die-cuts, and most of the page decoration. Small stickers and other accent pieces do not have to stay with these colors, but do be sure to match the "warm" or "cool" palette you are using. Organize your supplies, paying special attention to the way the colors work together and how you can use color to accentuate the focal point of your page.

## Contrast with Mats

There are two simple ways to draw attention to an element on a scrapbook page or to any work of art: 1) make the item very light or very dark 2) set the object off from the background by making it contrast with areas around it. These techniques are easy to use with the color trios listed above. If a photo you want to feature is very light overall, mat it with one of the very dark colors in your trio. Conversely, very dark photos can be set off with a pastel mat or a mat cut from a muted light color such as ivory, beige, or pale gray. As you complete your layout, make sure any very light or very dark areas are ones you truly want to stand out.

Consider these other color principles as you finish your layout:
- Colors appear to be brighter when placed next to black, white, or their complementary color.
- Dark colors are low key and convey heavy, serious,or depressing moods.
- Light colors are high key and denote light, airy, or mystic moods.
- Warm colors advance and signal excitement.
- Cool colors recede and reflect calm feelings.
- Gray and other neutrals take on some of the hues of colors next to them.

## Unity

Unity is created through balance, consistency in choice of design elements, and through repetition. Balance and style consistency have already been discussed. Repetition of colors, lines, shapes, or any other design feature is an additional way to create unity. Patterns lead the eye along the line of the repeating design elements. This way of directing attention gives a design movement or energy. Without it, a page seems stale or lifeless. Color is one of the easiest design elements to repeat. A punched yellow bow here and yellow mat there combine with the yellow dress in a photo to create movement and unity on a page. Choose one element of you layout and use it three or five times. Notice how it pulls the spread together.

Experiment with your colors and photos. Use some double mats of one light and on dark color to really bring attention to a photo. Remember to use color to balance you layout as well. Dark colors are heavier, as are bright colors. When you are with the colors, balance, and unity of your arrangement, mount everything on your page.

## Trios Chart

(Choose colors that are warm *or* cool, not warm and cool mixed)

**Warm**
Red, Orange, Yellow
and Ivory
are easiest to use together

**Cool**
Green, Blue, Violet
and Cool Gray
are easiest to use together

### Analogous Trios

**red/orange**
warm pink, brick red, rust
brick red, peach, ivory

cool pink, burgundy red, black
cool pink, burgundy red, white

**yellow/orange**
gold, golden brown, rust
golden brown, peach, rust

2 tints of light yellow, cool brown
ice yellow, white, cool gray

**red/yellow**
warm pink, brick red, gold
warm pink, golden brown, gold

2 tints of cool pink, cool brown
cool pink, ice yellow, white

**yellow/green**
gold, warm lt. green& dk. green
gold, golden brown, olive green

cool brown, mint green, pine green
ice yellow, mint green, pine green

**green/orange**
lt. country green, peach, ivory
olive green, peach, rust

mint green, pine green, black
mint green, cool gray, white

**blue/green**
turquoise, warm lt. green, ivory
turquoise, teal blue, and
lt. country green

ice blue, mint green, cool gray
ice blue, navy, pine green
navy, mint green, pine green

**green/violet**
lt. country green, plum
olive green, plum, ivory

mint green, lavender, deep violet
pine green, lavender, deep violet

**blue/violet**
teal blue, plum, ivory
turquoise, teal blue, plum

ice blue, navy, deep violet
navy, lavender, deep violet

**red/violet**
warm pink, brick red, plum
warm pink, plum, ivory

cool pink, lavender, deep violet
cool pink, burgundy red, deep violet

### Complementary Trios

**red/green**
warm pink, brick red, and
lt. country green
brick red, lt. country green, and
olive green

cool pink, mint green, pine green
burgundy red, mint & pine greens
cool pink, pine green, cool creme

**blue/orange**
turquoise, peach, rust
turquoise, teal blue, peach

ice blue, navy, white

**yellow/violet**
gold, golden brown, plum
gold, plum, ivory

ice yellow, lavender, deep violet
cool brown, lavender, deep violet

These combinations are very tricky, even with muted colors:
orange & violet and the triads (blue, red. yellow & green, orange, violet)

As you view the example pages, adapt the ideas that appeal to you for use in your albums. Let the colors, themes, and subjects in your photos guide you as you design your own layouts.

For very special photos, use simple layouts so the pictures stay prominent. The color scheme of the first layout is analogous.

Photographs by Linda Boyd, Busath Photography.

There are no rules about how many photos to place on a page; however, if you choose to use several make sure that the busy effect is what you want. The trip depicted on these pages was a very busy, exciting time. This layout uses the complementary colors of red (pink) and green in a Floral and Lace style. The Victorian stickers are from The Gifted Line, John Grossman, Inc. and the flowers are a color laser copy of actual pressed lilies of the valley.

The three layouts at the bottom of this page all use monochromatic (one color, sometimes in several shades or tints) color schemes. The violet pages use the Art Nouveau style by incorporating photocopied clip art frames. Many of the layouts in this book use clip art, most from books by Dover Publications. The stickers in the graduation layout are from Mrs. Grossman's Paper Co.

The family tree above is a simple layout using oval double mats. The parents and grandparents are pictured as young adults and as I remember them when I was growing up. The top right layout uses a gentle complementary color scheme of muted red (pink) and green and is an example of the Fantasy style. The fairy clip art as well as the airy look of the colors, embellishments, and photos give this appearance.

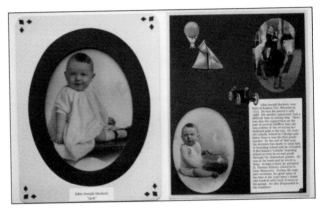

The baby layout above is a simple Victorian design. The ovals were cut with an oval mat cutter by Alto's EZ Mat to avoid cutting the photos. The Victorian stickers on this layout, and all the layouts on this page, are from The Gifted Line. Notice how the stickers are used to balance the pages. When a small element is needed to create unity or balance, a sticker or small punched shape can work wonders.

Monochromatic color schemes enhance older photos. The pink matting is just a sheet of 8.5" by 11" cardstock cut in half diagonally. Because the color works so well with the ivory photos, it enhances them rather than detracting.

The dark green, embossed frame is from Keeping Memories Alive. The punched squares and overalled bears give it a boyish quality. The squares make the layout a mix of Victorian and Modern Art, but it works because it is so simple. The lower left layout includes a laser copy of the cover of a scrapbook made for my father by his grandmother - it's in my genes!

The top two layouts use the Contemporary style. In the first one, notice the selective use of deep red to draw attention to particular photos. The sticker bow is from Mrs. Grossman's Paper Co. The nurses training layout is unique because it is the only layout in the book using the tricky triad color scheme. Yellow (mostly muted), red, and blue are used. It works because most of the colors are soft and red and blue hand-tinting are present on the large portrait. The sticker is by Mary Engelbreit from Melissa Neufeld.

In the heritage album layouts pictured, most of the photos are oriented at right angles rather than tipped in a diagonal slant. Even the snapshots in these pictures have a serious, formal look in comparison with modern photos. The straight orientation and simple page adornments fit with these pictures. In the large portrait of the woman above, the delicate mat was created by first tracing the picture's shape onto a piece of peach colored card stock. Then fancy paper edgers were used to trim the paper just slightly larger than the photo. When placed behind the picture, only the fancy edges show. The stickers are from The Gifted Line, as are those in the layout below.

The layout above blends the Nature/Rustic style with the Victorian touch of stickers from The Gifted Line. The blue accents highlight certain photos and create movement on the pages.

The top left layout features complementary colors, paper from Paper Direct, and Mrs. Grossman's stickers. Analogous colors are used above with Paper Adventure's paper, bows from Mrs. Grossman's, and pansies from The Gifted Line. Below, a monochromatic color scheme is used and die cut shapes are by Ellison Craft and Design.

This page uses photos cropped to create a puzzle design.

This page is split by subject. Photos for a karate belt test coordinate with science project pictures in a blue and muted orange complementary color scheme.

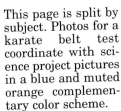

The layout of this family tree page was created on a computer and the photos were then cropped into ovals of the right size.

The tools at right are pencil and pen color keys. Mark on the charts with each one you have. They make it easier to choose the right pen or pencil, especially if you have a large collection. Titles were made with Lettering Delights font program. Below is a tool reminder as described on p. 67.

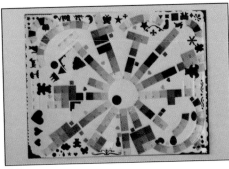

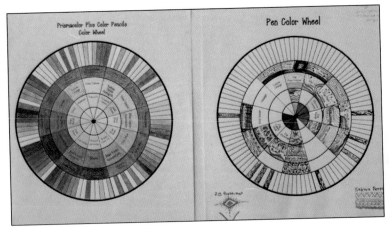

# Emphasis and Value

Again and again, I have asked you to consider where you want your scrapbook viewer to look on each page. This section will guide you in learning many ways to draw the eye to your focal point. The three general ways to create emphasis are:

- Singularity - The item is unique on the page. (A lock of hair is an example.)
- Contrast - Placing two unlike items near each other.
    light and dark values
    complementary colors
    large item and small item
    variety in number of objects in groupings
    simple object and detailed object
- Optical weight - These characteristics draw attention more than their opposites.
    large
    dark
    detailed
    bright
    numerous
    in front of another object

To create variety and interest on the page, be sure to include a lot of contrast. It is, however important to create a balance between unity and contrast. Too little contrast and a page is dull, too much and it is chaotic. The key is to choose what you want to highlight using contrast and then create unity around that focal point. Use the list under "optical weight" to decide how to emphasize a photo. If the picture is already oversized, it will draw attention due to its size. If you are cropping a photo that will be your focal point, be careful not to shrink it too much. You can give it emphasis by adding a mat that is large, bright, or detailed in relation to the rest of your page. If you will be overlapping photos, be sure the most important photo is in front.

## Value

Value is just the lightness or darkness of a color or object. Some colors, like yellow, have a light value in their pure form. Others, like violet, have a dark value. In mixing colors, adding black makes a color's value darker and adding white lightens the value. Most color groups in the Trio Chart were chosen to provide a wide contrast between the values of the colors. This makes a page interesting and allows you to use value to focus attention toward a particular place on the page.

Even though dark objects are visually heavy, giving a photo a dark mat will not always accent it. If the picture is dark already, it will just blend in. One of the best ways to be sure a picture shows up on a page is to give it a mat that contrasts with the value of the photo itself. If the photo pictures children playing in the snow, choose a darker mat to set it off. Choose a light mat to draw attention to a photo taken inside a cave.

For this practice layout, choose a collection of pictures that includes some photos that are light and some that are dark in value. Include at least one important photo that will be a challenge to highlight on your pages. It might be a smaller or darker picture or one that is important but must share a page with an attention-getting object like a laser copy of a child's drawing. Choose your paper colors, using the color trio chart if you want. Include one piece of pattern paper. Pattern paper has a lot of optical weight because of the details in the design.

## Patterned Paper

Most patterned paper is challenging to use without overwhelming your photos. Use these keys to keep your pictures prominent:

- Use one, or at most two, patterns per page for your first pages.
- If you use a large piece of pattern paper on your page, mat pictures that rest on top of it. A contrasting mat helps pull a photo forward so it does not get lost in the busyness of the pattern.
- Use the pattern paper for the lower layer of a double mat.
- Cut accent pieces, like a die-cut bow, from the patterned paper.
- Stretch one piece over the two pages of a spread.
- Use the examples below as a starting place for using pattern paper.

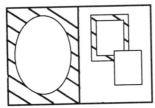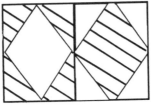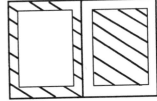

Two special cropping techniques can emphasize a photo with one primary subject. The first is silhouetting. Simply cut the person or subject out of its background. This gives a strong emphasis to that photo and usually works best if it is done with only one photo on a page. The second technique is a modified silhouette. This time most of the photo is cropped into a simple shape like a rectangle or circle, but a small portion of the subject hangs out of the shape and is cropped silhouette-style. It is also called "bumping."

If you choose to mat these specially cropped photos, a very simple, thin mat works the best. Especially with silhouette-cropped photos, it is important to ground them on the page. Place them behind a page element, such as another photo or a paper element, so they do not appear to float or drop off the page. (Unless, of course, it's a trampoline photo!)

Our final technique for creating emphasis also creates balance. It works best with a simple page and is the same technique used to place a subject in a photo. Use the rule of thirds. In the diagram, the page is divided into thirds horizontally and vertically. If you place an object on the lines, it gains emphasis and creates a balanced composition. It is much more interesting than positioning it right in the center.

Use value, emphasis, and the rule of thirds as you arrange your layout. Contrasting mats, detailed pattern paper, and special cropping techniques can also be used to emphasize important photos.

# Perspective and Intensity

Our final design concepts are perspective and intensity. Intensity was covered extensively in the color section. It is included here to give you a chance to focus on ways to use it in your layout design. Intensity, or brightness, is potentially one of the strongest ways to draw the eye in a layout. Think about the fluorescent papers available (I am not suggesting using them; just remember how they look). These colors are so strong that they grab the eye. For small punched accents or a fine line border, these might work on a scrapbook page. For the most part they would just be overwhelming. If you choose a very bright page decoration, make sure that you evaluate how it will effect the entire spread. A tiny bright sticker might be just fine, but a fluorescent green witch die-cut may push the Halloween photos into the background by contrast.

Besides the obvious use of intense colors to draw attention, consider the opposite use of intensity. If you want parts of your page to recede, or stay in the background, use low-intensity colors. This is quite handy if you want to create depth on your page. A muted background color with medium intensity mats and page decoration and bright photos seems to have dimension. Just as a page with all low-intensity colors is flat and boring, a page with all bright busy colors is monotonous because you don't know where to look. No matter what colors you choose, be sure to include a wide range of values or intensities to give the page depth.

## Dimension

For your last practice layout, choose photos that you want to arrange in a scenic page fashion. This means that the page will be decorated to replicate the location the pictures were taken. Photos taken on snowy hills, beaches, mountain areas, and forests trails lend themselves well to this technique. Before you begin to layout your spread, consider the ways to create the illusion of depth on a two-dimensional page. An object appears farther away if it is:
• behind another object
• higher on the page
• smaller
• grayer, bluer, or blurrier

You probably will use only one or two photos in the "scene" portion of your layout. It is fine to mount the others floating above it. Choose your colors for the background. Even though you will choose "sand" color or "sky" color for those elements, you still have a range of "sands" from which to choose. If your photos have a cool cast to them, choose a creme sand rather than a tan sand and vice versa if the photos are warm-toned. Start with your sky and build your scene from the background through the middle-ground and foreground. You may want to silhouette some photos and have the subjects sitting on the "sand." You could even place them partially hidden by a paper sand dune. Use your tips above to give the scene depth. Place the smaller photo of a child higher than the larger photo and the small one will appear to be further back. Have fun with this and don't be concerned about getting it "right." Play with the photos and shapes until you feel good about them and then mount them on the page.

You can also create a sense of depth on the page by weaving paper, using patterned paper and stationery, and by using sponging techniques. It is not necessary to try to create depth for every scrapbook page. If you use a good range of color values and other contrasts, your pages will be interesting and not flat. Special attention to depth is useful for some pages such as the scenic type just described.

## Top Tips Chapter 7

### General Design Principles
- Design your layouts in two-page spreads.
- Consider the preferences of the album owner when choosing a design style.
- Before working on a layout, choose the message and focal point for those pages.
- Select a design style for your layout and avoid supplies that clash with it.

### Borders and Line
- Decide whether or not to include borders in your design.
- Remember that the thickness and shape of a line conveys a mood.
- Use line to lead the viewer's eye, including the sight-lines of your photo subjects.
- Create border templates if you do a lot of borders.
- When using decorative scissors, or doing any delicate cutting, cut into the tight spaces. Pull the scissors away and go in toward the corner instead of in and out.
- Use a craft knife compass with a scrapbooking pen to create circle designs.

### Balance and Shape
- Create balance in your layouts by creating equal optical weight on each side of your design.
- Large objects can be balanced out with several smaller objects.
- The key to steady cutting with a circle cutter is firm pressure down to hold the paper or photo in place.
- Use a sharp blade and practice on scrap paper and spare photos.
- Make a circle cutter template if you need help centering your circles.
- To punch out uniformly spaced shapes for a border, use the center notch and back stop of the punch to line up your paper.
- Save symmetry, or formal balance, for single portraits or formal antique photos.
- Consider detail, such as the pattern in some paper, when you evaluate the optical weight of an object.
- Check your layout for balance and good design by looking at it upside down.

### Unity and Color
- Lay your photos on several colors of paper before choosing which to use.
- Choose colors that allow your photos to shine, if they are your intended focus.
- Use very bright paper to highlight journaling pages, newspaper clippings, and other less interesting page elements.
- Use bright colors for small accents such as stickers, punched shapes, and pen lines.
- Select colors that coordinate with the warm or cool tones in your photos.
- Explore the color combinations in the Trios Chart.
- Use contrasting color mats to enhance your photos.
- Create unity in your design by repeating elements such as colors.

## Emphasis and Value
- Use singularity, contrast, and optical weight to emphasize key photos.
- Pick colors that contrast with the value of your photos to make them stand out.
- Select pattern paper to add detail, but use it selectively to avoid busyness.
- Silhouette some photos for emphasis.
- Ground silhouette-cropped photos by overlapping for best results.
- Use the rule of thirds for pleasing placement of objects on your page.

## Perspective and Intensity
- Use a variety of intensities and values on your pages to create interest and depth.
- Place an object behind another object or higher on the page to make it appear further away. If it is smaller and blurrier or grayer, it will also appear to recede.
- Weaving paper, patterned paper, and sponging techniques also create depth.

To get the most from this chapter, be sure to do each of the practice layouts. The tips may be useful, but design is learned by doing. By focusing your attention on just one or two design elements at a time, you will find that you easily master them and begin to use the principles in all your layouts. If you are very new to scrapbooking and design, consider going through the first four practice layouts twice to internalize the concepts. This chapter is intended to guide you as you discover your own style. It is not a list of rules.

The color wheel below may be copied and used to make a pen or pencil key.

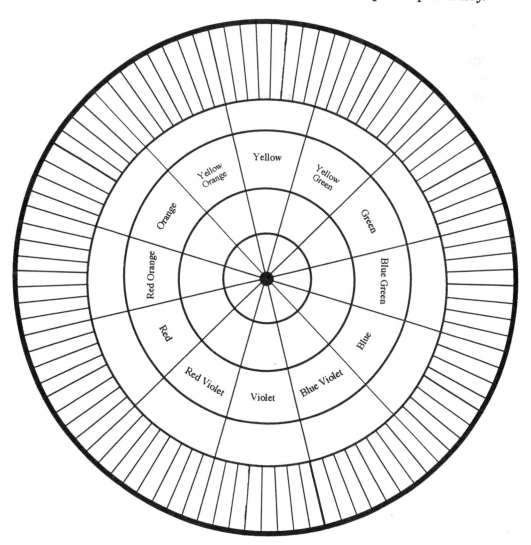

## CHAPTER 8

# Saga

### ❧ Tell the Stories

Scrapbooks are such a rich record of our lives because they combine so many means of expression. Photographs, newspaper clippings, letters, play programs, cards, certificates, and our written comments all may combine to tell the story. Throughout this book, the word "journaling" is used to refer to the words you write, or print out and mount, on your pages. These written comments are a vital and exciting part of your pages. When people are shown different scrapbook pages and asked which ones they like best, they usually select the pages with a lot of writing. If your time for scrapbooking is limited, consider shortening some of the elaborate design techniques and spending more time writing.

### Titles

Journaling takes many forms. The shortest type is a title: a simple message that highlights the main event or idea of the page. Many scrapbookers like to use clever titles on their pages and collect phrases for future use. Chatterbox Publications offers little books filled with these snippets and many scrapbooking Internet sites post collections of them. Song titles are particularly popular for page titles. Lyrics and perhaps an entire song can enhance your page. If titles appeal to you, keep a small file or notebook to jot down phrases you like. This suggestion is really for scrapbookers of all styles and preferences. If you have a place to record journaling, layout, and photo ideas, these fleeting thoughts will find their way into your albums and be your inspiration for further creativity. Make sure, however, that clever song titles or clichés don't dominate your albums. Important thoughts can't always be expressed with a snappy phrase. Title some pages but feel free to leave others with just captions or other writing.

### Captions

Captions are usually the simplest form of journaling. The answers to Who, Where, When, and What make an adequate caption. More complex thoughts and feelings enrich captions and lend interest to the page; however, they are not required. Just like cropping photos, aligning a photo on a mat, or any other skill, the more you write, the better you get. Make a point to write something for every two page spread and you will quickly find writing for scrapbook pages becomes easier, quicker, and more enjoyable. The results will be worth the effort.

### Story Bits

Many people are intimidated by writing paragraphs on their pages. Titles and captions are doable, but more than that feels like too much. Go beyond the who-what-when captions by writing what I call story bits. Rather than write a paragraph, write a few descriptive phrases or sentences. These thoughts can be a set of ideas that are only loosely related. On a page with a photo of my grandmother in her kitchen are the following bits:

"I got to snap beans, cut biscuits, and stir the batter."
"Every time my father visited, she made him a German chocolate cake."
"Mock apple pie from Ritz crackers, Sunny Delight, and tiny bottles of Coca Cola."
"Chicklets, *The Edge of Night*, fried okra, and afghans always remind me of her."

## Narratives

Narratives are just stories. If you want to get more comfortable adding this type of writing to your albums, try this strategy: Sit down with a good friend, a tape recorder, and one of your albums (an old photo album will work, too). Turn on the recorder and start looking at the album and tell your friend about the events pictured. You may even forget about the tape recorder after a while. Enjoy making those memories come alive for yourself and your friend. Later, listen to the tape. Make some notes if you want to, but just listening and then writing freely may feel best. This technique also can be used to create an audio record to accompany your album. You may be surprised how much you will learn if you record the recollections of an older relative.

# Journaling Helps

You may not realize how much written information you have for your albums lying around your home. Letters, diaries, school papers, and computer files may provide you with pre-written journaling. Print out those letters to your mother, your annual holiday letters, and the statement you sent to the insurance company after the auto accident (which wasn't your fault). You may not put all these papers on your pages, but they may spark some memories. What is your goal? If it is to tell your stories in interesting, easy, and vibrant ways, consider using everything you have.

If you would like to include more "meat" in your journaling, consider some memory ticklers. The bibliography contains several books which will provide you with questions to get you thinking. One of my favorites is *The Castle of the Pearl* by Christopher Biffle. You write your way through an adventure that takes place in a castle. If you want to write more, but find yourself stumped when you sit down to do it, you may enjoy this process. Some of these books are designed to fill-in; others contain lists of questions and other suggestions to get you writing.

## Handwriting, Lettering, and Computer Use

Use what works for you to enjoy writing for your albums. Although I agree that the inclusion of your own handwriting enhances your albums, it is not a required element. Because I prefer word-processing, I include a handwritten compiler's note at the end of each album I complete. In it, I express my feelings about the people and events in the photos and my experience of creating the book. After dutifully providing a sample of my own handwriting, I write captions and narratives to my heart's content using my computer. For the snazzy lettering look, I usually use Inspire Graphics' Lettering Delights.

If you make a mistake when you write on a page, cover it up with opaque ink, a sticker, a punched shape, a photo, or a title written on cardstock and then mounted over the goof. To reduce mistakes, write titles and captions in pencil and then trace over the letters with a pen.

I am learning to enjoy lettering a little more. Lindsay Ostrom's *ABC's of Creative Lettering* is a great course in how to have fun making letters. To help you get started, two basic lettering styles are illustrated here. The popular dotted alphabet is very forgiving. The dots give your letters a finished appearance. If a letter is off a little, make a bigger dot! The double-ended pens made especially for scrapbooking work great for these letters. Draw the bodies of the letters with the thin tip and then dot them with the thick tip. For the most attractive spacing, write out the entire title or caption and then add dots or other embellishments. Notice that the letters are not written on a straight line. Purposely bounce your letters up and down (one higher, next one lower, higher, lower, etc.), This casual look avoids the problem of words slanting up or down and still has a finished appearance.

ABCDEFGHIJKLMN
OPQRSTUVWXYZ

abcdefghijklmnopq
rstuvwxyz

To quickly center your title on the page, write it out on scratch paper first. Count the letters to find the middle letter and place that one in the middle of your title space. Finish the title by writing forward to the end and backward to the beginning. Use your scratch paper title to keep your place. Do this trick in pencil and then write over it with pen. Writing backwards with pen may cause you to drag your hand over a letter and smear it. If you do a title off-center, add a sticker, doodle, or punched shape to the end or beginning to create a balanced look. Draw your letters; don't write them. The lower case "b" is a circle and a straight line, the "x" two diagonal lines. Pay attention to giving your letters nice round circles and straight lines.

When you have mastered dot letters, explore this versatile alphabet. It is simple and the letters can be filled in with a theme that fits your page such as hearts for romance or snowflakes for winter.

## Memory Help List

For some aspects of our lives, we have no photos. A great way to include these events in our scrapbooks is to write about them. Use this list to help you recall key periods of your life and notice which experiences inspire you to write. It may also remind you to take those "forgotten" photos or to save clippings that tell your stories. Be sure you include in your albums all issues that are important to you. If it is important to you, your children and grandchildren will benefit from knowing about it.

A key challenge for almost 20 years of my life was managing my body fat, eating, and fit-ness. I came to be passionate about taking a healthy approach to these issues. My private album is filled with Oprah Winfrey articles and other magazine clippings that expressed my attitudes or made me angry. Pages with skeleton-thin models and crazy weight-loss schemes (with my outraged comments written in the margins) are also in that album. This struggle is reflected in the pictures of me in our family albums, but without these clippings the story of my experience is missing. Political cartoons, clipped advice columns by Ann Landers and Dear Abby, and political commentary by Molly Ivins also fill my pages.

In recording my own life, I am much more a compiler than a journal writer but I manage to do some of both. Remember to include the humorous side of your life as well. Funny clippings and the written record of children's amusing comments make a great read. One day, out of the blue, my son said to me, "guess what?" Of course I replied, "what?" "That's what!" was his surprising response. He had just told his first joke! If I had not jotted it down on a calendar, I might have forgotten it entirely and I would certainly have lost the detail that it happened when he was barely two years old. My other son loved to sit on the bottom of a special posture stool and "type" on the seat - his "peputer." This memory, and others such as him reading the book *The Hobbit* when he was only eight years old, gives a window into what was important to our family. These collections give me pleasure as I review my life and attitudes and I believe they will benefit, or at least entertain, my descendants.

**Firsts**
steps
haircut
bike
joke
day of school
job
car
home
Christmas tree

**Events**
dances
reunions
weddings
crises
elections and political events
military or church service
injuries and accidents
promotions
awards
moves
vacations
camp
graduation

**Day to Day Life**
your city, town, or county
bedtime
bathtime
quiet times
toilet training
special toys
best friends
sleepovers
chores
pillow and water fights
"boo-boos"
snow

pets
picnics
lessons and practicing
clubs
place of worship
cooking and baking

**Yearlies**
signature
what I'll be when I grow up
goals
height and weight
prices of common goods
headlines of the year
sayings and jokes
first day of school

**Favorites**
song
joke
TV show
movie
dinner
dessert
hobby
book
teacher
subject
poem
toy
game
recipe
fad
hangout
quotations and sayings
entertainer
author
hero
painting

season
flower
color
holiday
sport
animal
restaurant

**My Favorite ABC List**
A - aunts, autumn, airplane
B - bath, baby, beach
C - cat, camping, Christmas
D - Dad, dog, dancing
E - Easter, eat, exercise
F - family, friends, farm
G - grandparents, gardening,
    games
H - house/home, Halloween, hats
I - imagination, ice cream,
    instruments
J - jobs, jewelry, jump
K - kitten, kiss, karate
L - leaves, library, letters
M - Mom, mail, me
N - neighbor, niece/nephew, naps
O - orange, outside, ocean
P - presents, painting, popcorn
Q - quiet, quilt, "quack" (duck)
R - reading, race, rocking chair
S - swim, school, snow
T - toys, tools, telephone
U - uncles, umbrella, upside down
V - vacation, vegetables,
    valentine
W - wagon, winter, wedding
X - XXX (kisses), xylophone
Z - zoo, zebra, zipper

# CHAPTER 9

# Shapes, Stamps, and Special Effects

Beyond the basics of effective borders, mats, and color coordination, you have various options for decorating your pages. The design exercises in Chapter 7 taught you simple uses of punched shapes, stickers, and die-cut shapes. In this chapter, you will find suggestions for creating more complex page accents. Remember that the best way to achieve attractive pages is by taking time to experiment with your tools and supplies. This is one of the best ways to use your paper scraps. When you explore with no goal for a particular page in mind, your creativity soars freely. You will be surprised at some of the great results. Save your experiments. Even if you are not sure how you will use an idea in the future, if you like the way it looks, keep it. Every so often pull out those "doodles" to see if they jog ideas for page layouts. Copy ideas from idea books or magazines, if you like, but be sure to give your own creativity a chance to come out and play as well.

Most of this chapter is devoted to die-cuts and punches because they are so popular, widely available, and able to create a wide variety of designs. Basic guidelines for using rubber stamps are included. If you choose to use them extensively, get more information from rubber-stamping stores, mail order catalogs, and Internet sites (www.intersurf.com/~redstic /R101/R101.htm and www.inconnect.com/~ginwood). More specialized tools and page effects conclude this chapter.

## Die-Cut Shapes

Die-cut shapes are images of animals, flowers, houses, and hundreds of other objects, cut from paper or cardstock. The shapes are cut with a special die-cut machine and metal dies that are mounted on wood with a foam layer added. They can be purchased individually or in packets from scrapbooking suppliers. Many scrapbook stores also have die-cut machines their customers may use for a fee or as a free service included with a paper purchase. This section includes hints on cutting your own shapes as well as ways to use them creatively in your layouts.

The primary way to get creative with die-cuts is to layer them. This means that you take one element of the shape, such as the cherries from a cluster of cherries, and cut it from two colors of paper. Then layer one on top of the other. In this example, cut the whole shape from green and cut just the berry part from red. Then glue the red cherries over the green cherries and you have red cherries with green leaves. Most of the layering and cutting ideas below will be most useful to those who have access to a die-cut machine. Another option is to order from the suppliers who offer custom die-cuts service. The customer chooses the shape and the paper and the company cuts and ships the shapes made-to-order.

## Hints on Cutting

1. Plan ahead for your time using the machine. Have a list of shapes to cut and pre-cut paper stacked up, in order, ready to use. If you are limited to using the machine for a short appointment time, go before your appointment and look at the shapes (usually displayed on a bulletin board in scrapbook stores), take notes and buy your paper. You may even want to precut your paper to die-cut sizes. Most shapes measure 3" to 5" inches in width, except for jumbo shapes.

2. Dies cut shapes by pushing on the paper with a sharp edge until the metal cuts through. This makes the shape slightly curved so it has a definite front (edges curved down) and back (edges curved up). When using one-sided patterned paper, be sure the top side is facing the die before you cut. This is particularly important when layering so all the pieces will match up.

3. Never pump a die-cut machine. This does not make it cut through any better; it only wears it out faster. With especially complex shapes (swingset, ivy, insects, etc.), you may need to cut twice. Place the die with the middle of the handle over one half of the shape and press the handle down. Very carefully slide the paper and die so the handle is over the other half of the shape and press the handle again. For the roller type machines, if you can't get a clean cut you may need to place a thin piece of scrap cardboard between the wood side of the die and the tray and then run it through. This may provide enough contact to give a good cut.

4. For accent colors, you do not have to cut the entire shape from that color. This is a great way to use up scraps, especially if you have access to a roller die-cut machine. (You can see exactly where you have placed the paper on the die when using a roller machine.) In the cherry example above, you need only a scrap of red paper large enough to cover the cherry portion of the shape, not the leaf part as well.

## Layering Hints

1. Keep one bottom layer shape whole to use as a base for the finished product. This is the paper that all the other pieces are mounted on. It is either the color that will show the most or the outer edge color (such as the ruffle on a frilly bib, the rays on the sun, or petals on some flowers).

2. Get some good, sharp scissors. The ones with smaller 1.5" blades work well for cutting die-cuts apart.

3. For the sharpest look, trim the bottom layer in a little before you glue a piece over it. The green cherries had their edges chopped off before the red cherries were glued on. It is usually quicker to trim off edges than to meticulously match the edges as you glue layer upon layer.

4. Keep your overall goals for your pages in mind before getting carried away with layering. A finished die-cut layered with several bright colors becomes, in effect, a giant sticker. It draws a lot of attention to itself on your page. Consider experimenting with softer colors. Use fancy layered shapes to accent important journaling on pages with photographs, or use them on title pages or other pages with no photos at all. This way your snazzy die-cuts will not outshine your photos.

## Specific Layering and Decorated Die-Cut Ideas:
### Flowers, Fruit & Veggies

These are simple: just make one green shape and one flower/fruit colored shape, cut them apart and layer. The scored lines give you easy cutting guides to add more dimension. For the daffodil, cut shapes from green, a lemon yellow, and a soft butter yellow. Cut the "trumpet" from one yellow and mount it on the center of the other yellow flower. Next cut off the yellow "leaves and stem" and trim the edges of the green flower portion a bit. Finish by gluing your layered flower on its green stem and leaves. Use the same approach for cherries, tomatoes, and most flowers. Consider using muted greens and some softer colors for a more elegant and realistic effect.

### Perforated Shapes

Bibs, diaper pins, award ribbons, hamburgers, and anything with a bow are examples of perforated shapes. These are easy because the layering lines are "drawn" on for you by the perforations on the shape. Simply choose two or more colors, cut on the dotted lines and layer the smaller parts over the larger base die-cut shape. You can use patterned paper too. It looks great for bib ruffles, hat bows, baby blocks, and country-style accents. Don't limit your layering to shapes with scored lines, though; once you prove to yourself that you can layer, it becomes easy to see the shapes within the shapes that would be improved by using two or more colors.

### Shadows

Try this technique with trees, balls, leaves, ballerinas, birds, people, and stars. Shadows can be created in at least three ways:
1) The single shape is the shadow. An example would be to cut the shape of a girl praying using maroon paper and mount it slightly overlapping a white box with a pink mat. In the box, write the little prayer you say with your child and use photos of your bedtime ritual and the sleeping child to finish the page. A black bat can be set off-center over a large yellow circle moon. Place a dark green fir tree border at the bottom of a piece of soft-colored outdoorsy paper.

2) Cut the shape and its shadow. Layer a colored ballerina over a slightly angled gray shadow. Back an orange jack-o-lantern with yellow paper to "glow," and mount it over a black shadow on blue-gray background paper.

3) "Float" shapes over their shadows. This works best with a simple shape like a heart or tree. Cut a shadow of the same shape in a color slightly darker and duller than the background paper on which you plan to mount it. Cut hearts from mauve patterned paper. Cut the shadow hearts from maroon and mount them on dusty rose background paper. A brown basketball with a black shadow mounted on gray paper with motion lines drawn in really creates the illusion of movement. Tan bears with dark blue shadows will seem to float on slate blue paper. These techniques can also be used with punch outs, especially larger ones.

## Mats

You can mat any die-cut shape, but the simpler the outline the easier it is to cut a mat. If you are a perfectionist, you can use a quilter's 1/4" disc (available at fabric stores for about $1) to trace around smooth shapes and get a very exact mat, but it won't go into tiny corners. Matting is a great technique to use when you want a shape to frame journaling or a title. Cut a golden yellow apple and add a red mat behind it to frame "Back to School" or "Spelling Bee Winner." A pink teapot with a lavender mat can announce "Tea Party Birthday." Mat a pink shell with a beige-over-tan double mat to set off an important title such as "First Date - Beach Party!" or "Mommy, it looks just like snow! - First trip to the Gulf Coast." Mats also can be used with the shapes themselves. Mount a firecracker with its star burst on yellow and then on white for a bright effect. A red over gold over white sun looks hot! Simple shapes like hearts, gingerbread men, balls, flashes, eggs, and simple animals lend themselves best to matting.

*Licensed Designs © & ™ Ellison*

Blocks, ice cream cones, party hats, simple houses, and beach balls can be layered even if you only have one of the die-cut. These shapes have one part that is simple enough to trace and then cut out by hand. One side of the block, the cone, roof of a house, and pompoms are easy pieces to cut. You can cut parts to layer at home for these, even if you did not "cut to layer" when you cut (or bought) your shapes.

## Finishing Touches

Decorate shapes with punches, drawn lines, stickers, and even other die-cuts. Put leaves on the tree trunks, flowers in the pot or in the grass, or the dog in the doghouse. How about apple frames holding wallet photos of school friends on a large tree trunk? A puppy (or one of Mrs. Grossman's sticker critters) can splash in a wading pool, and an upside-down fishing hat can hold jumping fish. Look for other clever combinations that match your message. For country music fans, have a cowboy at the bottom of a page, a moon at the top, and a hand-drawn lasso rope from the cowboy to the moon. Title: "She thinks he can rope the moon."

Punches can be used to accent die-cuts. One of the simplest ways is to create a repeating pattern, like polka dots. Draw evenly spaced diagonal lines on the back side of the shape. Then draw lines going the other direction so you end up with roughly the same size diamonds evenly spaced all over it, then punch at the junctions of the diamonds. You can gauge where to punch by eye, but drawing the diamonds will give it the more even look of patterned fabric. After punching, mount the punched shape over the same shape in the color you want the dots, hearts, flowers, or stars to be. Use this method to decorate bows, blocks, presents, diapers, party hats, and teapots. For more random or multi-colored decorations, like cupcake sprinkles, it works best to punch out the shapes and glue them on. If you find it difficult to put adhesive on some tiny shapes, back the paper with double-sided photo tape before you punch it, peel off the backing paper, and mount the shape.

*Licensed Designs © & ™ Ellison*

Remember you can easily draw accents on shapes: eyes on animals, veins on leaves, spots on a dog, or stripes on a tie. If you are willing to use a bit of metallic ink in your albums, give the pencil die-cut a silver eraser grip,

the paint brush a metal bristle holder, or the crown some fancy touches. Pen-stitching around or on the shapes creates a country charm look on a page.

### Crimping Shapes

The previous techniques give primarily an illusion of texture. The paper crimper creates literal texture. Some clever crafter discovered that a paint tube squeezer corrugates paper. Since then, larger-sized crimpers have been created just to add this finishing touch to paper projects. Crimping a few shapes is fun. Suns, leaves, bows and simple animal shapes work well to crimp. If you want to get very detailed, crimp just part of the shape: the ridge that holds the bristles in the paint brush, the bottom edge of a carousel, or the handle of a screwdriver. On scrapbook pages, a little crimping goes a long way; be selective as to what you crimp. Also, make sure the crimped shapes are not denting the opposite page with their raised edges.

### Center of Attention Shapes

Some shapes work especially well for elaborate layering. Save these to accent a title page, a journaling-only page, or a page with important memorabilia with a dull appearance (a simple certificate for an important award, a church bulletin, or large newspaper clipping). They can also be used to enhance a page documenting a special event for which the photo turned out poorly.

The wedding cake, castle, elaborate house shapes, ballerina, ocean liner, tree house, crown, hot air balloon, and train work well for extensive layering. Remember, if you have access to a roller type die-cut machine, you can actually cut photos with dies. Reserve this for times when photos do not turn out well so it won't matter if the shapes overwhelm the subject of the photos a bit. For example, when our Christmas pictures were not so great one year, I cut them into holly leaves and made a wreath of photos, two colors of green holly leaves, punched red berries, and a red bow.

## Punches

Craft punches provide a variety of creative options for designing scrapbook pages. Three types of punches are available. Shape punches come in several sizes and dozens of shapes. Hand-held punches cut out tiny shapes such as several sizes of round dots, hearts, and teardrops. Corner and border punches are used to decorate the edges of mats or pages with repeating designs and fancy lines. Punches may be used to punch out shapes to mount on a page or to punch the design from the mat or page itself.

### Tips

Tracey Isidro, author of the book *Punch Happy*, has explored the usage of punches for scrapbooks for maximum fun and variety of design options. She recommends using long craft tweezers when layering punches to create designs. Glue sticks are her adhesive of choice, though she prefers a thicker glue applied with a toothpick when she is layering complex images such as wreaths. Other options for mounting punched shapes include the tape runner, double-sided photo tape, two-way glues, and the use of self-adhesive paper to punch out the shapes. Many scrapbookers recommend lubricating punches by punching through waxed paper or paper rubbed with soap and sharpening them by punching through very fine sandpaper or aluminum foil. You can also lubricate punches with a silicone spray and then punch through scrap paper several times to clean the punch. These techniques also work with fancy-edged scissors. Be careful not to overuse the sharpening suggestions so as not to wear out the edges of the tools.

Tracey has used her many punches extensively and does not sharpen or lubricate them. One reason she has not found this to be necessary may have to do with her punch technique. She frequently stands to work so she can easily put more pressure on the punch. If the punch is used "cleanly," with a pressure moving straight down, there should be less wear and tear. A punch cuts paper by pressing a positive image shape through a negative image hole. If the two parts move in a straight line, you will have less metal hitting metal as the punches are used. Detailed punches should also be easier to use with a straight punch motion. Tracey suggests using a piece of wood, or even the bowl end of a wooden spoon, to cushion the impression of the punch on your hand as you punch out the shapes.

## Versatile Punches

When you're getting started, it can be challenging to decide which punches to buy first. Tracey suggests the following punches as being most useful for a variety of layouts in your books: heart, star, circle, bear, and apple. Other geometric shapes, spirals, and leaves are also very handy to have. She suggests passing on specialized shapes such as the helicopter and dinosaur unless they have some special significance for you or a family member. Small punches work well to decorate the corners and borders of mats. For the cutting and layering ideas below, Tracey recommends using the large punches.

### One Shape, Many Objects
The following shapes transform into a variety of decorative items.

**Heart** - In addition to the variety of uses for hearts themselves, you can cut them to make strawberries, flower petals, leaves, and animal faces, among other things.

**Star** - A star can be a sheriff's badge, a clown collar, or leaves to top a strawberry.

**Apple** - Jack-o-Lanterns, vegetables such as peppers, and dog and cat faces and the obvious school theme are all options with the apple punch.

**Egg** - Flower petals, Christmas lights, and insect bodies are possibilities for creative extensions.

**Spiral** - An interesting abstract design for borders and accents; confetti, mouse tails, clown hair, and vines can all be created with spirals.

**Circle** - Circles, and all geometric shapes, are among the most versatile punches. Look around your environment to see how many things are obviously made up of simple geometric shapes. Experiment with these to make flowers, insects and other animals, Christmas tree decorations, balls, cookies, clowns, and buttons.

Leaves and bears complete Tracey's recommendations to buy first.

Bears become an amazing variety of things when she gets hold of them. My favorite is her child in a bear suit. Punch out a skin colored bear and a brown bear. From the brown bear, punch a face opening with a 1/4" round hand-held punch and trim off the "hands." Glue the brown bear on top of the "skin" bear and draw in facial features and a vertical line down the torso for the suit opening. She also turns the bear into a baby by trimming the ears off a flesh colored bear. Add a diaper cut from a white punched bear shape and a bib from an egg shape that has a scoop neckline punched out with the 1/4" circle hand-held punch. Bear becomes a gingerbread boy when the ears and toes are trimmed off and some opaque marker icing is added. Several other punched shapes can turn into holiday cookies when punched from cookie-colored paper and decorated with the opaque ink icing. Information about Tracey's book, *Punch Happy*, is on the last page of this book.

## Rubber Stamps

Stamped images can be used to create beautiful and interesting effects on scrapbook pages. If you make other paper crafts, such as greeting cards, you may want to assemble a collection of rubber stamps. If you will use them only for album pages, consider how many times you will use a particular image before purchasing a stamp. Hearts, flowers, and other objects that work well for borders and repeated designs may provide you the most benefit for your investment. With a cute fairy or bear that you will use only once or twice, you may be better off using clip art to photocopy or trace to add to your page. Some scrapbookers enjoy using a set of alphabet stamps to create titles on pages.

Rubber stamps are uniquely suited for creating certain effects such as sand dunes or grass tufts or the delicate look of a fern border. To achieve those looks, stamps may be your best choice.

To avoid the chance of the ink running due to moisture, and for more fade-resistant designs, use a high quality pigment ink with rubber stamps. Dye-based inks will not last as long. These stamp pads can also be used to create the paper texture effects described in the next section. For best results with rubber stamps use these suggestions:

1) To get a solid image, tap the stamp on the ink pad several times and then stamp with a good pressure. Do not "wiggle" or "rock" the stamp on the page.
2) Use your pigment pens to draw color on the stamp and then press it on the page.
3) If the ink begins to dry on the stamp, "huff" on it (blow out moist air as you do to dampen an eye-glass lens to clean it) to freshen the ink before stamping.
4) Clean stamps well between uses. If you are stamping a dark color after a light color, you may not need to clean the stamp in between.
5) Use a large flat eraser to reverse the image on the stamp. Stamp the design on the eraser and immediately use the eraser to transfer the image to your paper.
6) Explore the effects of overlapping stamped designs in several colors.
7) Use self-stick notes to mask part of the design to give the illusion of

two objects overlapped. Stamp the first design. Cover the part of the image that will appear to be on top of the second image with a self-stick note. Then stamp the second item over the mask. It will appear to be behind the first object.

8) For an interesting effect and a durable image, emboss your design. Sprinkle embossing powder over your freshly stamped image. Lift the edges of the paper to create a funnel effect and carefully pour the powder back into its container. A fine layer of powder will adhere to the ink. Heat the underside of the paper with a heat embossing tool and watch the image turn shiny and distinct. Embossing only works with pigment inks.

9) Pigment ink can be set with a heat tool even if you are not embossing. This will make it last even longer.

10) Keep your embossing tool away from your photos and be sure stamped images are very dry (heat setting accomplishes this quickly) before place them inside a sheet protector. Without embossing, pigment ink can take hours to set completely.

## Textured Papers

Use pigment ink pads for use with rubber stamps, or your pigment ink pens, to create lovely textured looks on your paper. These decorated papers may be used as the album page itself, or to cut mats and other additions to the page. The first three of the following ideas are from Kathryn Schein. You can see illustrations of these, and many other clever design ideas (including Tracey Isidro's work), on Kathryn's Web site, Scrap Happy (www.telepath.com/bcarson/scrap_happy).

### Plastic-Wrap Texture

Apply harmonious colors to the plastic-wrap with an ink pad that has removable sections (Colorbox makes these) or with a pigment ink pen. Crumple the wrap to distribute the ink and then dab it on the paper. The result is a fine texture in which some areas appear to be slightly raised. By experimenting, you can use this method to create delicate, bold, or rustic effects.

### Cosmetic Sponge Stamping

Draw a simple design, such as a flower, snowflake, or swirl on a new, clean, slightly damp cosmetic sponge with a pigment pen. Stamp the image on the page. You can make several imprints before re-inking. Each one will be a little fainter than the last giving a soft, watery effect. Overlap the images and try this with a variety of color combinations.

### Faux Water-Color

Mark with a pigment pen on a small plastic lid or glass dish to deposit a small supply of ink. Dip a slightly damp paint brush in the ink and quickly paint simple designs, such as flowers, on the paper. Be sure the brush is not too wet or the paper will warp.

A similar technique works beautifully to create a colorful sky background: dampen a white paper towel and wring out all the moisture that you can. Dab the towel on a pigment ink pad, or ink from a pen deposited on a plastic lid, and then tap off some of the ink on scrap paper. With just a little color left on the towel, swirl the soft color on the page to create the look of a watercolor sky. Use pinks and peaches, in addition to blues, to give the page a sunset effect.

### Stencil Effects

Stencils can be used with pigment ink pads and sponges to create a variety of effects. Stencils are available in cloud shapes for sponging an "airy" sky. Mountain stencils can be used to sponge a landscape; or foreground texture, in the form of blades of grass, can be added to a page. Checkerboard pattern stencils, purchased or hand-cut, are used to create a strong pattern. Remember to use your punches to create stencils yourself. A border of hearts in various reds and pinks can be sponged around the edge of a page using a handmade heart stencil, ink pad, and sponge. For soft effects, with little visible sponge edge in the pattern, sponge the ink on with a small foam ball. An elegant effect is achieved by sponging ink on a page over a paper doily. If you sponge color onto a white page, it looks just like there is a white doily on a colored page.

Stencils can be used with media other than ink. Trace inside the stencil design with colored pencils and then color in some of the areas. Use a regular pencil to trace the design and then go over the pencil lines with a pigment pen. Paints and other products that are photo-safe and appropriate to use in your albums may also be available for use with stencils.

### Free Form Backgrounds

Colorbox pigment ink pads are specifically designed to apply color directly to the paper, in addition to their use with rubber stamps. This technique creates expressive paper to use for cutting mats. Hold the pads with the little handles on their undersides and stamp the color on your page. You can create a very regular, repetitious design, or a random collage of color. Consider which colors work well together, especially if they will overlap. Complimentary colors will blend to a muddy hue if applied on top of each other.

### Art Air Gun or Air Brush Tool

This device consists of a small plastic bulb attached to a pen holder. It is used to blow ink off a pen tip onto the page. The effect varies with the force of pressure on the bulb, the distance of the pen from the page, and the angle at which you hold the gun and pen. The spray effect can be used alone or in combination with the stenciling techniques above. This is definitely a tool that works better with experimentation. Use a pen with a large tip, if possible, and do not tighten the tool against the nib too tightly or you will damage it. If the pen splatters more than you like, shift the angle so the pen is almost horizontal. Follow those guidelines and then just play. Discover the variety of effects available with a mini-air brush.

## Papercutting

Elegant, bold, and old-fashioned looks can all be achieved with papercut designs. A fun and simple way to try papercutting is with simple snowflake designs. *Snowflakes Made Easy* by Cindy Higham offers a variety of easy-to-cut appealing designs. For a simple page layout, mount a white snowflake on medium background color, mat photos on a coordinated dark color, and mount them on top of the snowflake. Or sponge over the snowflake on a white page as described previously with a doily. Use stencils to trace designs on paper and then cut them out with tiny Scherenschnitte scissors or a mat knife.

"Peek-a-boo" pages can be created by cutting a window from one scrapbook page to reveal a portion of the page below it. Use of this technique needs to be planned carefully because it involves four pages: the one before the window, both sides of the window page, and the one after the window.

Papercutting by Allison, a family-run business, offers a wide selection of patterns for cutting which vary in difficulty from easy to advanced. Their address is in the resource appendix. *The Book of Paper Cutting* by Chris Rich is also a good resource.

## Pop-Ups

A popular variation of papercutting is creating pop-ups. These are three-dimensional paper creations to add to your pages. If you use albums with adjacent pages right next to each other (no gap as with ring binders), the pop-ups may be fashioned to open up when a page is turned. Otherwise, they will need to be opened out on the page itself. If your pages are bound in the book by your sheet protectors, you can still add small pop-ups to your pages. Slip a piece of cardboard in the sheet protector and carefully cut out a window, the size of your pop-up, with a mat knife. *The Pop-Up Book* by Paul Jackson gives complete directions for many variations and the Web site, The Pop-Up Pages (www.firstascent.com/popup.html) gives instructions for several simple designs. The directions for two simple pop-ups are included below.

The easiest pop-up requires just three folds: 1) Fold the base paper in half. 2) Fold the top corner of the fold over to create a triangle shape. 3) Open the paper and push the folded corner inward. Now attach your photo, or other decoration, on the pop-up and mount the base paper on your pages.

The second pop-up is just a decoration with tabs that is folded in half so it will close up.

For the best results with pop-ups, score your fold lines before folding them. Using a ruler to keep the lines straight, trace over them with an embossing stylus. Assemble some practice pop-ups in old coloring books to get the positioning just right before mounting pop-ups in your albums.

## Dry Embossing

This subtle and elegant technique impresses a raised design on your paper. Any stencil that is not too thick may be used, but well-made, brass embossing stencils work best. If the embossed design is not going to be mounted directly over a photograph (on the edges of a window-cut frame for example), rub your paper with wax paper first. On a light box, position the paper with the waxed side up over the stencil. Gently trace the stencil design with an embossing stylus. Experiment with paper scraps at first since it is easy to tear some papers by pressing too hard with the stylus; however, the technique is very easy. One trick for working with dark papers is to position the design in a corner of the paper. Line up the stencil with the corner and trace the design with a pencil on the back side of your paper. Flip the stencil around to the front of the paper, again aligning it carefully with the corner, and use your penciled guidelines to trace with the stylus.

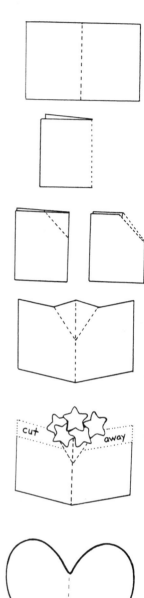

# Part III

# Extra Resources

# CHAPTER 10

# *Side Roads*

## ❧ *Extras to Explore: Videotapes, Audio tapes, Heirlooms, & Genealogy*

As you collect the items to include in your albums, you will probably discover that there are keepsakes you want to preserve that don't fit in your books. Many of the principles from Chapter 3 apply to almost any item you want to preserve as long as possible. Keep items clean, and store them in dark, dry, cool places. Keep them away from acidic and chemically active substances. Beyond these principles, there are some specifics that will help you best preserve your memories. Some media require special attention.

## Videotape

Videotapes offer you the opportunity to capture the sights, sounds, and movement of an experience. The medium is very different from still photography and requires attention to other elements. To get the best videos; remember that the tape records *your* movement as well as that of your subjects. Especially when you zoom in for a close up, stay very still to avoid distracting jerkiness in the tape. Because your subjects will usually be moving, avoid any unnecessary movement on your part. Use the zoom prudently, so the shifting view does not detract from your subjects. Use similar restraint in taking panning shots. They are great for capturing sweeping landscapes, but a little panning is usually enough; too much is dizzying. Plan your shots before you turn on the camcorder. Think about the event you are going shoot as if it were a Sunday newspaper cartoon. Visualize the scenes that will set up the action and tell the beginning, middle, and end of the story. Vary your shooting angles and listen to the sounds your camcorder picks up. With a little planning and attention, your videos will capture your experiences in rewarding ways.

Videotapes require special attention to make them last. Realize that if you play videotapes, they will eventually wear out. For your most treasured home movies, be sure to make a copy to keep and do not play it often. Then when the viewing copy becomes worn out, you can make a new viewing copy. Play the archive copy about once a year. On tapes you plan to keep indefinitely, break off the "record" tabs so the tape will not accidentally be recorded over. Use quality tapes in good VCR machines. Check the machine by playing another unimportant tape before playing your special videos. Keep your tapes away from motors and magnetic fields. Store them away from your television set. Rewind tapes completely, or play them to the end; don't store them partially rewound.

## Audio tape

Take the same precautions with audio tapes as suggested for the preservation of videotapes. With the availability of video sight and sound films, many people don't even consider making audio recordings anymore. Consider for a moment why you keep taking still photos. Why don't you record everything with videotapes? Perhaps because there are great advantages to limiting your attention. Notice how you sometimes feel as though you really *look* at a person for the first time when you study his photo. Capturing the sounds of someone's personality in audio recordings offers the same advantage. Tape your children's voices or the family singing together. Record the spoken memories of elderly family members or a speech your child will give at school. A wonderful way to encourage a young musician is to record a practice session about once a month. It will amaze you and your child to hear the difference between the early playing and the performance after a few months of practice. Explore the fun you can have with audio recordings.

## Heirlooms

A wide variety of objects can be treasured as heirlooms. I suggest that you photograph any objects that harbor special significance for you. This provides a record that you will have if the item deteriorates or becomes lost. After making a photographic record of it, consider the best way to store and maintain the object. Many heirlooms are textiles. Wedding gowns, quilts, needlework, and many items of vintage clothing are precious to us. Keep the article as clean as possible and don't expose it to anything that will make it deteriorate more quickly.

If it is strong enough to wash, use Orvus paste (available from preservation suppliers) to gently clean the cloth. Use no bleach or starch. If you dry clean, choose a cleaner who specializes in antique garments. Air out textiles that are too weak to withstand cleaning. Do any required repairs with a ball-point needle (to push the threads aside rather than tear them) and match the thread to the fiber of the item. For example, use cotton thread for cotton garments. Place as little stress as possible on the fibers. Hanging will generally put too much stress on parts of the clothing. Store the item flat, or rolled if it is too large. Wrap it in cotton or paper to protect it, and keep it in a cool dark place. Even safe plastics will trap moisture and should not be used to wrap heirloom textiles. Cedar chests may keep pests away, but the same vapors that repel insects deteriorate fabric. Avoid storing textiles around wood.

## Genealogy and Family History Research

Chapter 6 provides a brief introduction to family history research in the Heritage Album section. Gathering basic information from your relatives may be all the research you want to do. If you choose to do more, many resources are available. Just as this is great time to be a beginning scrapbooker, new genealogists have advantages which were unheard of ten years ago. Computer programs to help organize information, Internet access to huge amounts of information, and thousands of helpful genealogists anxious to share information are just a few current advantages. The genealogy sites mentioned previously are the best readily available resources. If you want only a few basic forms to complete, Stevenson Genealogy Center and DOTS sell simple pedigree charts (family tree, parental relationships chart) and family group sheets (complete record of a family, including parents and children). If you have a computer and plan to share your information with any other family members, investigate genealogy programs such as Family Tree Maker. The simple versions are sufficient if you expect to do little research beyond your family members. If you decide to do more extensive research, write down everything and be sure to record the source for each piece of information. This practice alone will save you frustration and back-peddling in your research.

## Journals

Just as still photographs and audio tapes focus attention in particular ways, so does a journal focus the mind. Journals assist you in learning more about yourself and in unleashing your creativity. This written record provides a unique insight into the mind of the journal-keeper for those who read it later on. If keeping a journal appeals to you, make time to write at least once a week. Buy a book of personal history questions, or get some off the Internet, if you need some help getting started. Keep writing a positive experience by doing it your way. Just as their are no rules for scrapbooks; there are no rules for journals.

## Framing

Hanging photographs is wonderful for decorating your home. As recommended previously, if you want to display your favorites, have extra copies made to keep in your albums to protect them from fading. To make your photos on display last as long as possible, use acid-free mats, and make sure the photo does not touch the glass. Plexiglas blocks more harmful light rays than glass, and metal frames present no danger to photos. If you do not have another copy of an important photo, display it for a limited amount of time. Avoid displaying photographs in locations that are hit directly by the sun in and humid locations such as kitchens and bathrooms. Because Fuji papers perform so well in tests of prints on display, consider this paper for prints that will be framed.

## Top Tips Chapter 10
- Keep all keepsake items clean, and store them in cool, dry, dark places.
- Take photographs of possessions that have special significance.
- Store videotapes completely rewound and away from motors.
- Make a copy of special videotapes for viewing.
- Explore the unique record you can create with audio tapes.
- Store textiles in acid-free paper and away from wood.
- Use on-line resources, or a simple genealogy book, to guide you as you learn this rewarding hobby.
- Frame your photos with acid-free mats, Plexiglas, and metal frames to make prints last as long as possible.
- If you frame your favorite photos, get extra copies to store in albums.

# Chapter 11

# Serious Subjects

## ❧ They Deserve a Place in Your Albums

Birthday parties, holiday celebrations, and graduation days are the subject of most families' photo albums. These events also deserve a prominent place in scrapbooks, but they are only one aspect of life. If your goal is to create a record of your life, or to express who you are, a wide range of experiences must be included in your albums. The serious side of life provides rich resources for meaningful pages.

Many scrapbookers create memorial pages to tell the stories of beloved ancestors who have passed away. These pages are an important part of the family history record. Most of us will deal with the death of a loved one several times in our lives. Feelings of grief, love, and admiration for a deceased friend or family member are worth including in our books. There is so much to learn from the experiences of others; a record of how one person dealt with a challenge may become a source of strength and inspiration to another.

Some experiences need to be recorded but are so private that you don't want to put them in a family album. A Private Album is the perfect place for many thoughts, feelings, and keepsakes. Love letters, a note of praise from the boss, or a sad poem copied down when a romance ended are meaningful items that fit best in a Private Album. Keeping the book for your eyes only gives you permission to include anything you want. This can free you to express your deepest feelings.

Journals are addressed briefly in Chapter 10. This book is not about journal-keeping. It is about collecting, compiling, and presenting a collage of items (including your written words) to record experiences and express messages. In some ways, an album can be a richer record of a life than a journal. The photos, artistic choices of color, and embellishments express emotions and personality that words alone cannot. This is not meant to diminish journal-keeping in any way; I highly recommend it. The avenues of creativity offered by scrapbooks, however, provide a unique opportunity for self-expression.

Feelings and personalities are at the heart of the serious aspects of memory albums. Anything you include that reveals those elements of your subjects enhances your album. Many times, written words are the best way to accomplish this. When my mother was a young woman, she was criticized by some of her elders for "going her own way." Despite the disapproval of her aunts, she went to Atlanta to begin training to become a nurse. For a young woman in South Carolina in the early 40s, this was a radical move. Once, when her father was particularly aggravated with her stubborn determination, he said, "One of these days, you're going to come up against a log you can't crawl over!" Her reply was, "That's all right. I'll just go around it."

More than 25 years later, a few months after my father's death, my grandparents spent Christmas with us. When they had a moment alone, my mother tearfully said to her father, "Daddy, I think I've hit that log I can't get over." As he put his arm around her he replied, "That's all right, Sugar, you'll find a way around it." In the few lines I wrote after she told me that story, those two wonderful people come alive on my album page. Listen for these stories that capture a slice of your life.

An essay written by my older son is an important addition to his album. One of his more unusual talents is his ability to contort his body in such a way that his feet rest behind his head. In the fall of 1996, he auditioned for a job in the Halloween show at a local amusement park. When he placed one foot behind his head and began to juggle, he ended up with more than a job. This is not one of his most commendable abilities; his accomplishments in debate, art, and academics are exceptional. The feet-behind-the-head talent, however, landed him on the front page of the newspaper (in color), and featured on the ten o'clock news on three television channels. The photos from the newspaper photographer, newspaper clippings, and tickets to the amusement park make up an amusing scrapbook layout. The addition of Jared's thoughts about the experience, and what is valued by society (as expressed in his college admission essay), make it a meaningful page.

Be selective about which serious subjects you include in your family albums, but don't restrict yourself too much. If it is important to you, it will be important to others. These stories may provide more than insight to readers. The story of a car accident may be just what is needed to persuade someone to fasten their seatbelt. Some challenges, such as recovery from an injury, can be rewarding to photograph. The patient has a concrete record of how far she has come since the incident. Other challenges, such as a chronic illness, may be documented through get-well cards, written comments, and photos of care-givers who have been especially helpful to the patient.

Use your pages to speak to your family. Don't miss the opportunity you have in making an album to tell your family members how much you love them. Let your pages reflect the sweetness, strength, or cheerfulness that you appreciate in a child or spouse. Be thoughtful as you write your messages. I saw a page titled, "Of course I'm cute-it's my job." Because the child pictured was a baby, I think the sentiment was amusing and appropriate. Being cute and appealing is part of babyhood. If that title were chosen for an older child, it might send a completely different and limiting message. Avoid titles that impose characteristics on children.

When you title a page, or write a caption, consider more than entertainment value. Make sure your words express thoughts you want a child to internalize. I like to ask my sons how they felt and what they thought during the events pictured on our album pages. I would rather write about my son being pleased with his performance in a karate or debate contest (and why) than my feelings about his accomplishment. Consider what messages you want to send and create your pages with those important thoughts in mind.

CHAPTER 12

# "Smile! Say Cheese!"

## ❧ How to Take Great Photos

Photographs are the star attraction of most scrapbook pages. If the pictures are good, the page will usually be appealing. This chapter is designed to give you the most basic instruction required to take good photos. Remember, sometimes the simplest techniques make the most difference. If you hold your camera steady, move in close, and make sure nothing distracting breaks up your background, you eliminate the causes of most really poor photographs. Suggestions for learning more about taking good pictures are provided at the end of this chapter.

### Cameras

In choosing a camera, you have four general types from which to choose. The most popular choice is a Point and Shoot or "PhD" (Push here, dummy) camera. It is highly automatic. On the least expensive models, the focus is fixed. The picture will only be in focus if the subject is within a certain range from the camera. Much more flexible are the automatic focus cameras. These cameras adjust in order to bring the subject in the view finder into focus. These cameras also make other automatic adjustments based on lighting and film speed. You have a degree of control, but if you just pick up the camera, open the lenses cover, point and shoot, there is a good chance you will get a photo with decent lighting and an in-focus subject.

### SLR-Single Lens Reflex

With this camera, what you see is what you get. The scene in the view finder will be the image you get on the finished photo. These cameras provide the most flexibility to the photographer and require the most expertise. Models are available that work automatically when that option is selected while allowing the user complete control with the manual setting. A camera like this is a good choice for amateur photographers who want to learn more.

### APS Advanced Photo System

While both cameras above are 35mm and are structurally similar, the APS is an entirely different system. It features drop-in film loading, negatives stored in cartridges, and many fool-proof composition features. Consider using one of these only as a second camera. This system has several disadvantages and some unknown factors. Film processing is less readily available and costs more. The film is one-third the size of 35mm film so enlargements are grainy by comparison. The longevity of these negatives, stored in the case as they are, is unknown and so is the longevity of the system itself. It may become more popular; it might not. If the system became unavailable, using the APS negative cartridges to get reprints could be a problem.

## Polaroid

Polaroid photos have the preservation disadvantage of retaining the processing chemicals in the finished prints. For this reason alone, consider a Polaroid as a fun second camera if you have one, but do not rely on it for your long-term photo record of your family.

## Film and Camera Hints

Be sure to choose a camera with which you are comfortable. If you do not know how to use the features, you may as well not have them. Read the camera booklet completely and do your best to practice using the features on everyday shots. When you take a few photos of your child with her favorite doll to finish up a roll, try out a feature at the same time. If your camera will adjust for backlighting, pose your daughter in front of a brightly lit area, select the backlit feature and take the shot. This will help you learn about your options. Then you will be most likely to think of them automatically in photo situations which require a particular feature to get the best shot.

Remember the basic mechanics of cameras. Carry fresh batteries with you at all times, and buy another spare set as soon as you put your spares in the camera. Choose a camera with a zoom lens if you want to be able to get in close. I consider this an almost required feature photographing children. It enables you to get in close without intruding on what the children are doing. Another wonderful aid to getting great pictures is a tripod. This allows you to take better shots with low light, fast action, and close-up photos. If your camera has a timer, it will also allow you to be in group photos. The most basic mechanical consideration is to carry "camera insurance," because mechanical things will malfunction. For any really important events, carry an extra camera (a disposable will work) with you. If you lose, break, or forget extra batteries for your regular camera you still will get some photos of the event.

One of the most important keys to good photos is choosing film with an appropriate speed for your needs. The lower the number, the slower the speed and the better the conditions must be to get good photos. With ASA 100 speed film, the light must be bright and the subjects relatively still to take a sharp picture. This film will give the best enlargements because the grain is very fine. It is great for outdoor posed shots on a sunny day. For general use, ASA 200 or ASA 400 film is usually best. The new faster films, such as Fuji Super G 800 and Kodak Gold Max, are wonderful for taking photos in tricky conditions. For getting a shot of your graduate as he comes down the aisle of the auditorium or an action shot of your soccer player, these films are ideal. They are not good for enlargements because they come out very grainy. Experiment with the different film speeds to learn what works best for you and the photos you take. Try the low speeds for some outdoor portraits and keep the fast speeds on hand for low light and fast action situations.

Be sure your film is fresh when you buy it and use it long before the expiration date. Keep your film and camera cool and make sure you do not leave it in a hot car. Make sure the film is threaded properly when you load the camera. Be sure to look at the window that shows the number of pictures left on the film and listen when you take a photo. This will alert you if the film is not advancing properly so you can fix it. Be sure to choose quality processing at a lab that uses a long-lasting paper for prints and rinses them properly. Consider your need for copies and get duplicate prints if you will use them. They are cheaper than ordering reprints later.

All the photograph composition information is included in the Top Tip list for this chapter. Make a copy of this page, and keep it in your camera case. Look it over now and then to vary your photos and make them better.

## Top Tips Chapter 12

### Cameras and Film

- Choose a camera that you will be comfortable using.
- Read the manual and try out all the features on everyday photos.
- Always carry fresh batteries and, for important events, a back-up camera.
- Choose the best film speed for the photo situation.
- Use fresh film and keep it cool.

### Composition

- Keep your backgrounds clean and watch for objects "protruding" from your subject's head.
- Move in close and shoot some shots at your subject's eye level.
- Do not cut people off at the joints. Crop at midthigh or the waist rather than at the knees or the hips.
- Frame your subject with objects, such as tree branches, in the foreground.
- Explore different viewpoints; shoot from high, low, and off to the side.
- Remember to shift the rectangle; take vertical and horizontal shots.
- Tell the story by taking a sequence of shots.
- For sports, dance and other action shots anticipate the peak of action and be ready to shoot at precisely that moment.
- Use the rule of thirds. If your subject is placed on one of the lines in the illustration, the photo composition will be most pleasing.
- Be patient, practice, and take several shots for best results.

### Babies and Children

- Use a faster speed of film and natural light, especially for babies.
- Keep the camera handy to catch that special, unexpected moment.
- Use a zoom lens to get in close.
- Take monthly shots of babies, and annual shots of older children, in the same place with the same props.
- Blend in to the background or shoot while children are involved in an activity to get good candid shots.
- Include backgrounds, pets, and favorite objects that tell your child's story.
- Show relationships between siblings by catching their interactions on film.

### Groups and Portraits

- Ask your subjects to pose close together.
- Make sure that all the people are about the same distance from the camera.
- Use a tripod and a camera with a timer so you can include yourself in the photo.
- Shade, late afternoon light, and early morning light is most flattering.
- Use a fill flash (flash turned on manually) for outdoor portraits in harsh light.
- Fill the frame with your subject.
- Use the red-eye reduction feature or brighten the room to reduce red-eye.
- Angle the camera slightly down or come in from the side to limit red-eye.
- Experiment with taping a single sheet of facial tissue over the flash.

# CHAPTER 13

# Cyber-Support

## Scrapbooking Resources on the Internet

On-line scrapbooking services are rich sources of information, inspiration, and encouragement. The willingness of participants to reach out to help other scrapbookers is absolutely amazing. I have watched women come to bulletin boards and e-mail lists for comfort when they experience a loss. The responses posted were heartfelt and very thoughtful.

In another instance, two women agreed to make thousands of photocopies so over 200 scrapbookers could share layout ideas and handouts. Bickering and strong opinions about the "best" scrapbook supplies surface here and there, but they are the exceptions. If you are new to Internet use, there are a few basic tips and types of services you need to understand. Flip back to the glossary if you are not familiar with any of the terms used in this chapter.

### Scrapbooking Web Sites

Scrapbooking Web sites are locations you access with your computer. Type in the address, or URL, of the site you want to see, and your computer will take you to the homepage of that site. This page is usually an introduction to the site and a table of contents. It will usually have buttons or highlighted words that link you to other parts of the site. For example, click on the word "events" with your mouse, and you are transported to a list of scrapbooking shows and getaways. Click on "catalog," and the screen fills with products sold by that company. If you don't know how to already, be sure to have someone show you how to "bookmark" a site or a page on your computer. This process makes the page easy to access whenever you want to return to it. Simply go to the bookmark on your list and quickly connect to the appropriate site. Notice that you can bookmark a particular page you visit frequently, such as a message board, in addition to the homepage of the site. Many sites post a list of links to other scrapbooking sites. This is like a public list of bookmarks. As you visit sites via a link page, add bookmarks for the ones you like. One of the best scrapbook sites to visit first is Vicky Sedgwick's Scrapbooking Obsession. Vicky's link lists contain most of my top 20 sites and each listing is very descriptive. She is very aware of the sites available and even gives a "Site of the Month Award."

Another great site for beginners to the Internet, scrapbooking, or both, is Graceful Bee Online Memory Magazine. This site is very user-friendly and is filled with useful information and clever ideas. It's like a magazine, except instead of turning pages, you click on articles you want to read. Anna Swinney and Debbie Janasak have illustrated the articles with wonderful examples. One of their goals for the site is to be a "launching point for the creative talents" of their readers. In case you are curious, the name comes from the creators' names: Anna means "Graceful" and Debbie means "Bee."

Last in my set of great beginners' sites is the original scrapbooking Web site, Jennia Hart's The Scrapbooking Idea Network, or TSIN for short. Jennia's site offers a wide variety of resources: layouts, articles, product announcements, and message boards or bulletin board systems (BBS). For the latest information on new products, this is the site to check. Jennia is making product information a key focus of her site.

## Message Boards

Using a message board is a clever way to find exactly the information you need. When you visit a board, you will see lists of messages, usually arranged with indentations to sort the messages by threads, or topics of discussion. One person posts a question or comment and other visitors respond. Scrapbookers are usually very polite and friendly on-line, but it is still a good idea to read posts and sites with a lot of basic information such as Graceful Bee, before participating in these discussions. One board that has a lot of activity and is very friendly to beginners, is the Sidelines Board at Sara Anderson's site. The tone of the board makes it easy to jump in and participate in the discussions.

If you have trouble printing a post or other on-line information, remember that you can copy the text and paste it into a word processing document. For more help using your computer to create scrapbook pages, read the information posted at Scrap Happy and Graceful Bee. They will guide you in downloading fonts and clip art from the Internet. The Family Base and Inspire Graphics sites also offer information to help you with computer scrapbooking.

## Chats and E-Mail Lists

Some sites offer real on-line discussions via chat rooms. At these locations, you post a message and someone else visiting the site at the same time answers you. One other option for on-line interaction is e-mail loops or listservers. When you subscribe to these services, you begin to receive e-mails about scrapbooking from the people on the list. When you send a message to the list address, it goes to everyone on the list. Some lists offer a digest feature, which means that you daily receive all the messages in one big e-mail. This is convenient, since some lists generate dozens of messages each day.

Notice and abide by the guidelines for these different forums. Lindy Latta, a fellow list member, suggested most of the following courtesies. Most lists and message boards expect participants to stick to scrapbooking topics. Sometimes posting digressions is permitted if you label the post as a "tangent" ("tan.") in the subject line. Before you send a post, make sure you have updated your subject line to reflect the content of your message. Advertising, rudeness ("flaming"), and repetitious posts are not welcome. There are special boards for advertisements and for posting messages to your secret pals (your swap partner, as explained below). On e-mail lists, send replies of interest to just one person to that individual only - not to the whole list. When you reply to posts, the original post becomes part of your message unless you delete it. Retain a small part of it, if it makes your reply easier to understand, but don't include it in its entirety. One shortcut you will see on message boards is the posting of a short reply in the title of the post itself, followed by the letters "nft" for "no further text." For example, if someone posts the question, "which fancy scissors should I send to my sister who is new to scrapbooking?" you could reply, "deckle scissors-great for beginners! nft" in the subject line of your post. Learning the Internet on scrapbooking sites is a lot of fun. If you have a question or a problem, someone is sure to help you.

## Swaps

Lists and bulletin boards frequently feature swaps which readers may join. One popular type is a Secret Pal Swap. Usually, the coordinator of the swap will send a questionnaire to be filled out and returned by those interested in participating. The coordinator then selects pals for everyone and sends each person the questionnaire of their new secret pal. The pals send gifts anonymously for a while and then reveal their identities. Many on-line retailers advertise that they will ship to secret pals so your postmark will not give a clue as to your identity. Other swaps involve specific scrapbooking supplies. In a sticker swap you might send 20 modules of stickers, and your wish list ("flower and baby stickers" for example), to the swap sponsor. She collects all the contributed supplies and then sends them all back out again based on the requests. Paper, die-cuts, and punched paper shapes are also exchanged in swaps.

## Tips

As you explore different sites and revisit those you like, you will notice that some change frequently and others remain as they were on your first visit. After noticing which sites were most interesting to me, I organized my bookmarks into folders marked "weekly," "monthly," and "check occasionally." Sites I visit more than once a week are on my bookmark list, not in a folder. I have a separate folder for sites that are only on-line catalogs of supplies. (Such sites are listed in the Resource Appendix, not in this chapter.) As Myndee Reed of Scrapnet points out, two great on-line resources are contests and scrapbook supply sales. By posting messages on BBS, submitting layouts, or sometimes just sending an e-mail, you become eligible to win scrapbooking supplies in various contests. As you search for bargains, be sure to watch for shipping deals when you shop on-line.

A unique advantage with on-line services is the immediacy of updating information. As soon as an on-line store has new product, they can let you know. The information shared on the boards is also current. If Scrapbook Company X has slipped in its customer service, someone will probably mention it on a bulletin board. The reverse is also true. dMarie, for example, has built customer loyalty with quick service and personal attention. (It also doesn't hurt that she and her husband Mark have posted over 800 layouts on their site and are very helpful to those who post on their BBS.) As you enjoy the bonanza of goodies on the Internet, remember Vicky Sedgwick's advice for those new on-line: "Use your time on the computer wisely and then turn it off and scrapbook!"

# Top 20 List of Internet Scrapbooking Sites
(Most of these are on Scrapbooking Obsession's link lists.)

**Scrapbooking Obsession\*** - THE scrapbook link site, plus tips, sayings and more
www.geocities.com/Heartland/Ranch/2637

**Graceful Bee\*** - great articles and technique information; updated weekly
www.gracefulbee.com

**The Scrapbooking Idea Network (TSIN)\*** - new product information and more
www.scrapbooking.com

**Scrap Happy\*** - computer basics, design techniques, fonts, swaps, and more
www.telepath.com/bcarson/scrap_happy

**Sidelines\*** - active and friendly BBS, catalog, Ask an Expert, and layouts
www.saraslines.com

**dMarie\*** - great BBS, layouts, poems and titles ideas, and supplies catalog
www.dmarie.com

**Scrappers Anonymous\*** - stores, magazine index, events, links, sticker sales
www.computer-concepts.com/~scrapanon

**Two Too Cool Scrapbooking** - busy BBS, gets very heated sometimes; bookstore
www.rockower.com/bbs

**Jangle\*** - tip of the day, several BBS, contests, and a lot of current information
www..jangle.com

**Scrapnet\*** - events, quotes and sayings, links, contests and more; updated regularly
www.netprojections.com/scrapnet/scrapnet.htm

**Stampin' and Scrappin'** - several BBS, including an active consultants board
www.stampinscrappin.com

**Treasure Maps** - how-to site for genealogy, very beginner-friendly
www.firstct.com/fv/tmapmenu.html

**Cyndi's Genealogy Links** - amazing site with links to a zillion genealogy sites
www.CyndisList.com/photos.htm

**New York Institute of Photography** - photography lessons, updated monthly
www.nyip.com

**Abbey Press** - excellent pH test pens, paper preservation, list of permanent papers
palimpsest.stanford.edu/byorg/abbey

**Clarke Preservation** - Good, basic preservation information
www.lib.cmich.edu/clarke/pres.htm

**Library of Congress Photo Preservation**
gopher://marvel.loc.gov/00/services/preserv/info/photo.leaf
gopher://marvel.loc.gov/00/services/preserv/info/basics

**Scrap N' Post** - home of a scrapbooking e-mail list and the Scrap N' Post web ring
home1.gte.net/saraka4

**Ultimate Scrapbook Store Source** - list of over 600 sources of scrapbook supplies
members.aol.com/KPenman617/Storelist.html

**Oral History sites** - questions to help you with detailed journaling
www.rootsweb.com/~genepool/oralhist.htm
www.usu.edu/~oralhist/oh.html
www.familytreemaker.com/bio/index.html
www.genrecords.com/library/question.htm

**\* indicates sites with layouts**

The contemporary layout above features a laser copied tassel and ready-made journaling in the form of the invitation and ticket. More personalized journaling was included on other pages documenting the event. The "BHS" was cut from photos taken at a distance in the auditorium during the graduation.

The gardening layout displays the Nature/Rustic style with stickers from Melissa Neufeld.

The Modern Art style karate layout gives an illusion of movement due to the rings drawn with a scrapbook pen and a compass sold with an X-acto swivel blade craft knife.

The rings on the school photos layout are cut with a circle cutter. Cut a circle the size you want the ring to be, then cut out the center to make the ring. The Gifted Line small flower stickers accent the design. The lower school photos layout features an embossed mat from Keeping Memories Alive.

Most layouts on this page use only simple mats and a few stickers from The Gifted Line. The top wedding portrait is matted in a more elaborate fashion. An oval and a rectangle were traced onto a piece of cardstock and the oval was cut out with an oval mat cutter. (This could also be done with a craft knife.) The rectangle corners were cut out with straight scissors and then trimmed with fancy scissors, as was the outer edge of the mat. The outer mat was finished with a corner punch and mounted on dark paper. The corners were then mounted, leaving the centers free so the photo could be slipped under them. The matted photo was then mounted on black cardstock, emphasizing the corner punch design.

Letters, telegrams, certificates, and newspaper clippings provide documentation on the pages. These were either sprayed with deactification spray or photocopied onto acid-free, lignin-free paper. The little girl with a bridal veil card is from The Gifted Line. The hands holding flowers were illustrations in an out-of-print book. Similar designs are available from The Gifted Line.

Usually it is best to avoid repeating photos on a page; however, it works with these World War II newspaper clippings and the photo used in them. Notice the shadow mat used to set off the business card as well as the postcard and clippings in the layout at the bottom of the page. The confetti stickers above are from Mrs. Grossman's Paper Co.

For the Air Force duty photos, simple geometric accents are used such as the pinwheel arrangement of the photos over the plum colored paper shown at left and the square punched shapes below.

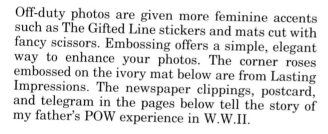

Off-duty photos are given more feminine accents such as The Gifted Line stickers and mats cut with fancy scissors. Embossing offers a simple, elegant way to enhance your photos. The corner roses embossed on the ivory mat below are from Lasting Impressions. The newspaper clippings, postcard, and telegram in the pages below tell the story of my father's POW experience in W.W.II.

The doily look above was created by sponging over a doily using pigment ink applied with a foam ball. When the doily was removed, the design was left on the white paper. The program page, above right, was set off with a punched lace mat. This was created with teardrop and micro-dot hand-held punches. Ready-made paper lace items, including photocorners, are available from Moments and from Pebbles in My Pocket. The die cut wedding cake and dancer are by Ellison Craft and Design. The flower stickers are from The Gifted Line.

The examples at right show ways to set off special portraits using circle and oval cutters to make the mats and punches to enhance them. The triangles are made with a square punch used at an angle. The patterned paper on the quilt page is from Northern Spy, as is that used for the

bow on the wreath below. Journaling may be added on ivory circles or octagons mounted in the empty spaces. The leaves of the wreath were cut with Ellison dies.

# Sources Appendix

## Scrapbook Resources

Many scrapbook supply companies are small, home-based businesses. Some are mailorder only, so call before stopping by a "store." Companies with an asterisk (*) charged a fee for catalogs at one time. Check on-line or by phone to get current information about a company's policies.

## Preservation Supplies

Abbey Publications
7105 Geneva Dr.
Austin, TX 78723
palimsest.stanford.edu/byorg/abbey
abbeypub@flash.net
512-929-3992   FAX 512-929-3995
pH test pens/ permanent paper info.

The Archival Company
P.O. Box 1239
Northampton, MA 01061-1239
www.archivalcompany.com
800-442-7576

Birth-Day Time Capsule Co.
800-530-7078

Conservation Materials Ltd.
1395 Greg St., Suite 110
Sparks, NV 89431
800-733-5283   702-331-0582
FAX 702-331-0588

Future Packaging and Preservation
800-786-6627
professional time capsules

Gaylord Bros. Archival Storage
Materials and Conservation Supplies
P.O. Box 4901
Syracuse, NY 13221-4901
800-448-6160   800-634-6307
FAX 800-272-3412

Hollinger Corporation
9401 Northeast Drive
P.O. Box 8360
Fredricksburg, VA  22404
800-634-0491   FAX 800-947-8814

Light Impressions
439 Monroe Ave.
Rochester, NY 14603-0940
800-828-6216   716-271-8960
FAX 800-828-5539

Original Time Capsule Co.
800-729-8463

Restoration Source
P.O. Box 9384
Salt Lake City, UT 84109-0384
rsourceslc@aol.com
801-278-7880   FAX 801-278-3015
Archival albums/conservation supplies

University Products
517 Main Street, P.O. Box 101
Holyoke, MA 01041-0101
www.universityproducts.com
800-628-1912   800-762-1165
FAX 800-532-9281

Wei 'To® Assoc. Inc.
21750 Mainstreet Unit 27
Matteson, IL 60443
708-747-6660
Deacidification solutions and sprays

## General Suppliers

C.W. Outlet
P.O. Box 164
151 East State Street
Lehi, UT 84043
www.scrapbooksupplies.com
801-768-8611   FAX 801-766-1066

Creative Memories
2815 Clearwater Road
P.O. Box 1839
St. Cloud, MN 566302-1839
www.creative-memories.com
800-468-9335   888-227-6748
direct sales through consultants

Creative Xpress!!/Provo Craft retail
295 West Center
Provo, UT  84601-4430
www.creativexpress.com
800-563-8679   FAX 801-373-1446

The Cropping Corner
3900 E. Mexico Ave., Suite 970
Denver, CO 80210
www.croppingcorner.com
scrapbook@croppingcorner.com
800-608-2467

*D.O.T.S™ ./I Love Remembering
Close To My Heart (scrapbook division)
738 East Quality Drive
American Fork, UT 84003
www.iloveremembering.com
800-965-0924  FAX 801-763-8188
direct sales and quarterly magazine

DMarie
187 Riverbank Ln.
Paso Robles, CA 93446
www.dmarie.com  dmarie@dmarie.com
FAX 805-227-7098

Exposures
1 Memory Lane
P.O. Box 3615
Oshkosh, WI 54903-3615
outlet store:
87 Water St.,
S. Norwalk, CT 203-866-5259
800-222-4947  800-572-5750

Keeping Memories Alive
P.O. Box 728
Spanish Fork, UT 84660-0728
Store: 260 N. Main, Spanish Fork
www.scrapbooks.com
800-419-4949  FAX 801-798-3420
retail & wholesale

Memories (formerly Memories & More)
www.memories.com
800-929-7324

Memories Direct
P.O. Box 1053
Fremont, NE 68025
www.mem-direct.com
info@mem-direct.com
888-860-8009  FAX 402-721-2845
volume discounts

*Memories to Cherish
7127 S. 400 W. #5
Midvale, UT 84047
801-566-4407  888-566-4407
FAX 801-566-4389

*Pebbles in My Pocket
P.O. Box 1506
Orem, UT 84059-1506
pebblesinmypocket.com
pebbles@pebblesinmypocket.com
800-438-8153
special orders 801-226-4434

Photo Crafts
P.O. Box 315
Yorba Linda, CA  92885
www.photocrafts.com
800-414-6419  714-993-3733
FAX 714-993-9796
huge selection-stencils, die-cuts & more

*Rocky Mountain Crafts
540 E. 500 N.
American Fork, UT 84003-1976
www.rmcraft.com
castellan@rmcraft.com
801-763-8628  800-270-9130
FAX  801-756-0577
eternal coupon available to get free
cardstock with minimum order

# General - Smaller Companies

Absolutely Everything
37 W. Main St.
Georgetown, MA 01833
absolutelyeverthing.com
800-464-0553

Bits and Pieces Scrapbook Supply
2302 Sword Dr.
Garland, TX 75044
www.register.com/scrapbook
bitsandpieces@sprintmail.com
972-496-6064 - voice & FAX

Country Sassafras
1124 First Street South
Winter Haven, FL 3380
members.aol.com/mgmh/index.html
mgmn@aol.com
888-552-5516

cutnfun Paper Craft Accessories
P.O. Box 1344
Goleta, CA 93116
www.cutnfun.com
cutnfun@silcom.com
805-685-8445 - phone & FAX
educator and consultant discounts

Eudemodia
322 S. Carolina Ave.
Booneville, NC  27011
www.eudemodia.com
HappyPeople@Eudemodia.com
336-367-3410
entertaining on-line catalog

Family Ties and  Family Trees
1397 E. Golden Cir. Dr.
Fruit Heights, UT 84037
801-546-9393

Fanatic Scrapper
6505 Foxhound Road
Knoxville, TN 37918
fanaticscrapper.dreamhost.com/index.html
fanatic-scrapper@mindspring.com

Heartstrings Network
378 Ivy Court
Pomona, CA  91767
home.earthlink.net/~heartstrings
heartstrings@earthlink.net
909-593-9902  FAX 909-596-0603

Memories and Milestones
1047 W. Sixth St., Unit D
Corona, CA 91720
pages.prodigy.net/smus/mm.htm
smus@prodigy.net
909-270-0212

Memories by Design
P.O. Box 962
Layton, UT 84041-0962
801-775-9380   888-SCRAP88
FAX 801-775-9320

*The Photo Safe
275 McShane Place
Monument, CO 80132
www.thephotsafe.com
info@thephotosafe.com
719-481-6224

The Photo Safe
1056 Caren Drive
Eldersburg, MD 21785
photosaf@erols.com
410-549-5211
volume discounts

Photographic Memories
1170 W. 152 Hwy Suite BB
Liberty, MO 64068
www.netprojections.com/photo/photo.htm
888-466-9003   FAX 816-466-9003

*The Price Cropper
1093 East Main St., #102
El Cajon, CA 92021
members.aol.com/pricecropr/HomeP.html
pricecropr@aol.com
619-593-7501

Remember Me
#103 - 250 Schoolhouse St.
Coquitlam, B.C.
Canada  V3K 6V7
www.remembermesb.com
mary@remembermesb.com
800-451-7086   FAX 888-558-6565
Rispy products

Scrapbooks 'n More
5769 Westcreek
Fort Worth, TX  76133
www.iboutique.com/starmaster
starmstr@ix.netcom.com
888-312-4449   817-294-4600

Scrap Patch
P.O. Box 645
Mendon, MI  49072-0645
www.iboutique.com/scrappatch/index.html
thescrappatch@mvcc.com

*Stampin'Up
Kanab, UT
www.stampinup.com   800-STAMPUP

Sunshine on a String
888-684-2665

# Specialized Suppliers
## Album Covers

Ravishing Wraps
801-225-8904
tapestry albums

Tapestry Umbrella
601 West 200 South
Smithfield, UT 84335
801-563-5757

## Die Cut Shapes

Albumania
286 N. 400 W. 112-3
Blanding, UT  84511
www.hubwest.com/albumania/ordering.htm
albumania@sisna.com
die-cuts and punches

Artistic Touches
378 North Main - Suite 101
Layton, UT 84041
801-543-3372
LDS themes

crafty cutter
179 Niblick Road, Suite 344
Paso Robles, CA 93446
805-237-7833

Dina's Die Cuts
3023 Hwy K Ste 590
St. Charles, MO 63304
www.dinasdies.com   dina@dinasdies.com
800-395-7583   314-980-2672

Katee's Kut-Ups
15864 Cumberland Drive
Poway, CA 92064-2345
katees@inetworld.net
619-748-4878   FAX 619-679-3262

## Paper & Papercutting Supplies

Best Way Imaging
6862 Chico Way NW
Bremerton, WA 98312-1024
www.bestwayimaging.com
info@bestwayimaging.com
360-698-1581   FAX 360-613-0340
Pergamano supplies

Meandering Paths
2005 E. 19th St.
Georgetown, TX  78626
lonestar.texas.net/~mcbee
meanderingpaths@sunbeltusa.com
254-869-7801

Paper Cuts (Lambson Lithographics)
246 N. Wenatchee Ave.
Wenatchee, WA 98801

www.papercuts.com
lambson@televar.com
800-661-4399   509-663-2839
FAX 509-663-8891
swatch books available

*Papercutting by Alison
P.O. Box 2771
Sarasota, FL  34230
941-957-0328   941-952-0763
amazing papercutting patterns & books

Twinrocker Handmade Paper
P.O. Box 413
Brookston, IN  47923
www.twinrocker.com
800-757-8946   765-563-3119
paper, papermaking/bookbinding supplies

## Stickers

*Memories and Milestones
1047 W. Sixth St., Unit D
Corona, CA  91720
pages.prodigy.net/smus/mm.htm
smus@prodigy.net
909-270-0212
discontinued stickers

Scapper's Anonymous
513 N. Adams
Grand Island, NE  68801-4441
www.computer-concepts.com/
~scrapanon/mailorde.htm
scrapanon@computer-concepts.com
308-384-4608

*Sticker Planet
10736 Jefferson Boulevard
Sticker Station 503
Culver City, CA  90230
www.stickerplanet.com
800-557-8678

Stickers Galore
3404 Meyer Place
Saginaw, MI  48603-2303
www.stickersgalore.com
ruth@stickersgalore.com

Stickers Galore!
2405 Forbes Dr.
Bellevue, NE  68123
www.vmap.com/stickersgalore
orbotet@msn.com
402-291-4208

Sticker Sensations
P.O. Box 2414
Denton, TX  76202
www.serve.com/stickers
batman@iglobal.net

Stickerville
Gentle Creations

1140 NW Lester Ave.
Corvallis, OR  97330
www.stickervilleusa.com/index.html
stickers@peak.org
800-682-3712   FAX 888-999-4568

Ticker Stickers
820 Main St.
N. Wilksboro, NC  28659
www.tickerstickers.com
tickers@abts.net
888-481-0117   336-667-0117

## Other Specialized Suppliers

Art2Art
P.O. Box 8370
Springfield, MO  65801
www.art2art.net
800-284-8195
light boxes & drawing boards

Associated Photo
800-727-2580
photo cards

American Bronzing Company
1313 Alum Creek Drive
Columbus, Ohio  43209
www.abcbronze.com
bronzeinfo@bronshoe.com
800-345-8112   614-252-7388

The Bronzery
441 W. Allen Ave. #105
San Dimas, CA  91773
www.bronzery.com
sales@bronzery.com
800-909-7523   FAX 909-592-3604

Bronzit - Baby Shoe Bronzing
c/o L. Bishop
1760 W. Rutan Road
Roankoke, VA  24012
www.bronzit.com
800-977-0374   540-977-3452

Carol Wright® Gifts, Dept. LL
340 Applecreek Rd., P.O. Box 8512
Lincoln, NE  68544-8512
402-474-1377
very inexpensive punches

Century Crafts
205 S. Puente St.
Brea, CA  92821
800-340-2031
Country Craft Kits for kids

*Connor's Collectibles
1346 Fayette St.
El Cajon, CA  92020
619-596-9092
panel templates, stencils, newsletter

Enterprise Art
P.O. Box 298
Largo, FL 33779
die-cut and embossed cut-out frame pages

Keepsakes Under Glass
www.keepsakesug.com
888-491-9940
glass cases

Loving Thoughts
3697 Oakridge Dr.
Bountiful, UT 84010
801-299-1813
Lasting Impressions embossing stencils

Miles Kimball
41 West Eighth Avenue
Oshkosh, WI 54906
920-231-4886
large selection of photo gifts

Moments
P.O. Box 3933
San Luis Obispo, CA 93403
805-541-3139
conservation sup./laser cut photo corners

Phantom Line Manufacturing Co.
955 Foothill Drive
Providence, UT 84332
mercury.digitalpla.net/~phantom
phantom@digitalpla.net
801-752-6590   FAX 801-752-6590
device reflects image onto page

Playing For Keeps
P.O. Box 1194
Glendora, CA 91740-7650
888-481-9459 or 626-335-7650
specialized album kits for young people

Precious Impressions
P.O. Box 50536
Provo, UT 84605
www.preciousimpressions.com
precimpres@aol.com
888-758-4611
castings of baby hand/foot

Stencils & Stuff
5198 TR 123
Millersburg, Ohio 44654
330-893-2499

Stencil Outlet
8002-STENCIL   603-942-9957

SpotPen
Box 1559
Las Cruces, NM 88004
505-523-8820   FAX 505-647-8786

Stevenson's   Genealogy Center
230 West 1230 North
Provo, UT 84604

800-374-7296   801-374-9600
FAX 801-374-9622

Sudberry House
Box 895
Old Lyme, CT 06371
www.connix.com/~sudberry
sudberry@connix.com
800-243-2607   860-739-6951
FAX 860-739-9267
wooden memory trays with glass tops

# Manufacturers and Wholesalers

Accu-Cut®
1035 E. Dodge
P.O. Box 1053
Fremont, NE 68025
www.accucut.com  info@accucut.com
800-288-1670   FAX 402-721-5778

Adhesive Products, Inc.
520 Cleveland Ave.
Albany, CA 94710
510-526-7616   FAX 510-524-0573
Memory Mount, Crafters Pick glue

Alto's EZ MAT Inc.
Ellensburg, WA
800-225-2497
mat cutters, including oval mat cutter

American Traditional Stencils
442 First New Hampshire Tnpk
Northwood, NH 03261
www.Amtrad-stencil.com
800-448-6656   603-942-8100
FAX 800-448-6654

B & V Publishing
4633 Cass St.
San Diego, CA 92109
www.bandv.com
customerserv@bandv.com
makes scrapbook kits sold at Costco

Black Cat Red Eye Pens
3410 Harney St.
Vancouver, WA 98660-1829
www.teleport.com/~bcat
bcat@teleport.com
888-272-4708

Boss - Rememberances in audio
800-760-SING

Burnes International
94 Rowe Street
Newton, MA 02166

C-Line
P.O. Box 1278
Des Plaines, IL 60018
800-323-6084

C-Thru Ruler Co.
6 Britton Drive
Box 356
Bloomfield, CT 06002
ccthru@aol.com
860-243-0303    FAX 860-243-1856

C.M. Offray & Son, Inc.
Chester, NJ 07930
www.offray.com
acid-free peel and stick ribbon

Canson-Talens, Inc.
South Hadley, MA 01075
FAX 413-533-6554
800-628-9283

Carr Albums
HB Group
North Smithfield, RI 02896
800-343-6290

CR Gibson
32 Knight Street
Norwalk, CT 06856-5220
800-243-6004    FAX 203-840-3319

Cut-It-Up
4543 Orange Grove Ave.
Sacramento, CA 95841
916-482-2288    FAX 916-482-1331

DMD Industries
1205 ESI Dr.
Springdale, AZ 72764
www.dmdind.com
800-805-9890
Paper Reflections - paper/bound albums

Ellison Craft & Design
17171 Daimler St.
Irvine, CA 92614-5508
www.ellison-inc.com/ellison.html
888-972-7238    FAX 888-270-1200

Family Treasures
24922 Anza Drrive, Unit D
Valencia, CA 91355
800-413-2645    FAX 800-891-3520

Fiskars Inc.
7811 W. Stewart Ave.
Wausau, WI 54401
www.fiskars.com
800-950-0203

Frances Meyer Inc.
P.O. Box 3088
Savannah, GA 31402
www.francesmeyer.com
800-372-6237

Fresh & Funky Stencils and Supplies
One Heart One Mind
10608 Widmer

Lenexa, KS 66215
913-498-3690

The Gifted Line
999 Canal Blvd.
Point Richmond, CA 94804
800-5-GIFTED (800-544-3833)
FAX 510-215-4772

Heiss & Co.
704-228th Ave. NE #733
Redmond, WA 98052
DJHeiss@aol.com
425-868-4686    FAX 425-868-3640
acrylic rulers and other supplies

Hiller Industies
631 North 400 West
Salt Lake City, UT 84103
800-492-5179    801-521-2411
FAX 801-521-2420
large selection of photo-safe albums

Holson Albums, Todd Holson Consumer Division
800-243-8633

Lasting Impressions
585 West 2600 South, Suite A
Bountiful, UT 84010
800-9EMBOSS    801-298-1979
FAX 801-298-1983
embossing stencils

Making Memories
P.O. Box 1188
Centerville, UT 84014
800-286-5263    FAX 800-263-7478
wholesale distributor

Marvy®-Uchida/Uchida of America, Corp.
3535 Del Amo Blvd.
Torrance, CA 90503
www.uchida.com
800-541-5877    FAX 800-229-7017

MBI, The Album People
2280 Grand Ave.
Baldwin, NY 11510
516-623-4687    FAX 516-623-4528

McGill, Inc.
131 E. Prairie St.
Marengo, IL 60152
800-982-9884

Melissa Neufeld
7068 Koll Center Pkwy #425
Pleasanton, CA 94566
www.melissaneufeld.com
neufeldm@rest.com
800-NEUFELD (800-638-3353)
FAX 510-417-0755

Memories Forever - Westrim Crafts
P.O. Box 3879
Canoga Park, CA 91313
Chatsworth, CA 91311
800-727-2727   818-998-8550

Mrs. Grossman's Paper Company
P.O. Box 4467
Petaluma, CA 94955
www.mrsgrossmans.com
mgpc@wco.com
800-429-4549

Northern Spy
P.O. Box 2335
Placerville, CA 95667
www.directcon.net/nspy
nspy@directcon.net
916-620-7430
background papers & stamps

Panodia
Sommerset, NJ 08875
800-821-9777
tape runner

Paper Patch
P.O. Box 414
Riverton, UT 84065
800-397-2737   801-253-3018
FAX 801-253-3019

Paper Reflections
DMD Industries, Inc.
1205 ESI Drive
Springdale, AR 72764
www.dmdind.com
800-805-9890

PDM Adhesives Corp.
Fayetteville, GA 30214
800-248-4583   FAX 770-461-8452
Sailor pens and Leeho glue

Pioneer Photo Albums
9801 Deering Avenue
P.O. Box 2497
Chatsworth, CA 91313-2497
www.pioneerphotoalbums.com
800-366-3686   818-882-2161
FAX 818-882-6239

RA Lang Card Company, Ltd.
P.O. Box 64
Delafield, WI 53018
800-648-2388   414-646-2388

Sakura of America
30780 San Clemente St.
Hayward, CA 94544

SandyLion Sticker Designs
P.O. Box 1570
Buffalo, NY 14240-1570
www.sandylion.com

Sonburn
P.O. Box 167
Addison, TX 75001
800-527-7505
booklet, Retailers Guide to SB Profits

StenSource International, Inc.
18971 Hess Avenue
Sonora, CA 95370
209-536-1148
stencils

Stickopotamus™ and EK Success
611 Industrial Rd.
Carlstadt, NJ 07072
800-524-1349   201-939-5404

Suzy's Zoo
9401 Waples St., Suite 150
San Diego, CA 92121

Tombow - American Tombow, Inc.
Norcross, GA 30093
800-835-3232

Webway/Antioch
P.O. Box 767
St. Cloud, MN 56302

Wubie Prints
P.O. Box 1266
Sandy, UT 84091-1266
801-256-0185   888-256-0107
patterned paper

# Storage

Platte Productions
6660 Sausalito Ave.
West Hills, CA 91307
818-992-0529
Crop-in-Style Scrapbook Tote

Cropper Hopper - Leeco Industries
8855 Cypress Woods Drive
Olive Branch, MS 38654
www.cropperhopper.com

Family Scrapbook Connection
1418 Milan Court
Livermore, CA 94550
510-447-5403
iscrap4m@pacbell.net
Markers in Motion pen organizer

Highsmith
800-544-4661
Acid-Free Corruboard®BASICS organizers

OakTree Essentials™
P.O. Box 1472
American Fork, UT 84003
www.valuquest.com/oaktree
dbrockbank@valuquest.com
801-763-9975
The Ultimate Scrapbooking Bag

Piece Keepers
P.O. Box 571515
Salt Lake City, UT 84157-1515
www.organize.me   bonnie@inquo.net
801-293-8038

# Books and Publications

Apple of Your Eye
P.O. Box 521984
Salt Lake City, UT 84152-1984
appleye@juno.com
801-582-SEED wholesale 801-485-4270
*Core Composition* book

Blushing Rose Publishing
P.O. Box 2238
San Anselmo, CA  94979-9803
415-459-2263
Victorian albums

Cedco
800-227-6162
Anne Geddes baby books

Chapelle Inc.
Box 9252 Newgate Station
Ogden, UT 84408
801-621-2777
idea books

Chatterbox Publication
P.O. Box 216
Star, ID  83669
www.chatterboxpub.com
208-286-9517
small books on journaling, lettering, and titles

Cianciolo Enterprises
17290 Astro Dr.
Big Rapid, MI 49307-9521
www.multimag.com/bus/familyhistoryorganizer
888-367-3461
publishes *Family History Organizer*

Colortree
P.O. Box 1285
Eastsound, WA 98245
972-239-7888   FAX 360-376-6160
Sonburn's *Scrapbooking Your Family Memories*

Craftrends/Sew Business -Primedia Magazines
3761 Venture Dr. Suite 140
Duluth, GA 30096
craftrends@aol.com
770-497-1500   FAX 770-497-0144
Ads 800-448-8819
Publishes *Snapshot Memories* -no subscriptions

*Creating Keepsakes* Scrapbook Magazine
P.O. Box 1106
Orem, UT 84059-9956
www.creatingkeepsakes.com
888-247-5282   888-224-8235

FAX 801-225-2878
Magazine, Idea Annual & other books

Creative Teaching
5824 Bee Ridge Rd., Suite 412
Sarasota, FL  34233
Stuf4Skool@aol.com
800-595-5767   FAX 941-379-2462
*Teach with Creativity* book

D.O.T.S™./I Love Remembering
Close To My Heart (scrapbook division)
738 East Quality Drive
American Fork, UT 84003
www.iloveremembering.com
800-965-0924   FAX 801-763-8188
quarterly magazine

Deseret Book
P.O. Box 30178
Salt Lake City, UT 84130-0178
801-543-1515   FAX 801-578-3338

*DJ Inkers
P.O. Box 1509
Sherwood, OR 97140
www.djinkers.com
800-325-4890 retail
P.O. Box 2462
Sandy, UT 84091
800-944-4680 wholesale
whimsical clip art, stamps and stickers

Dover Publications
31 East 2nd Street
Mineola, NY 11501-3582
800-223-3130   516-294-7000
FAX 516-742-6953
huge selection of clip art and other books

*Familyphoto* magazine
P.O. Box 53211
Boulder, CO 80323-3211
800-289-1976
wonderful magazine on family photos

*Hot Off the Press
1250 NW Third, Dept. LL
Canby, OR 97013
www.hotp.com
503-266-9102   FAX 503-266-8749

International Scrapbook Association
Intern. Scrapbook Trade Association
P.O. Box 295250
Lewisville, TX 75029-5250
scrapbkc@gte.net
972-318-0492   FAX 972-318-0491
excellent newsletters

Memorable Impressions/Stampington & Co.
22992 Millcreek, Suite B
Laguna Hills, CA  92653
714-380-7318
Stamping/scrapbooking annual publication

*Memory Makers* Magazine
Subscription Office
P.O. Box 7253
Bensenville, IL 60106-7253
303-452-0048   800-366-6465
FAX 303-452-3582
Editorial Office
475 W. 115th Ave. #6
Denver, CO 80234
editorial@memorymakers.com
www.memorymakers.com

Mt. Olympus Publishing
78 West 2400 South
Salt Lake City, UT 84115
mtoly@wasatch.com
801-486-0800
*Family Focused* and scrapbook stories book

The Paper Rabbit
2269 Honolulu Ave.
Montrose, CA  91020
818-957-2848   FAX 818-957-2849
*ABC's of Creative Lettering*

Potomac Studios
18725 Mt. Lock Hill Road
Sharpsburg, MD 21782-2034
members.aol.com/PotomacSt/index.html
PotomacSt@aol.com
*Scrap House Newsletter*, black and white

Proust Press
www.triggers.com
510-845-5551
*The Memory Triggering Book*

*Rubber Stamper* magazine
P.O. Box 420
Englishtown, NJ 07726-9983

*Santa Cruz Comic News*
P.O. Box 8543
Santa Cruz, CA 95061
newpaper of political cartoons, 24 iss./year

*Snowflakes Made Easy*
Cindy Higham
314 Gordon Lane # C11
Murray, UT 84107
801-262-2336   FAX 801-263-2533
book

Strawberry Patch
P.O. Box 52404
Atlanta, GA 30355
800-875-7242   FAX 404-841-9586
*Roses in December: My Life Story and Other Memories*, fill-in book

*Stuck on the Edge*
6401 14th Ave. S.
Richfield, MN 55423-1735
www.mninter.net/~rogerall
rogerall@mninter.net

612-861-4814   FAX 612-861-3734
monthly black and white sticker newsletter

Vermilion
P.O. Box 176
Cohasset, MA 02025
617-924-4760
publishes Donna Green's *To My Daughter*

Wasatch Mountain Design
P.O. Box 70171
Salt Lake City, UT 84170-0171
801-969-1808
*Lettering & Liking It* books

# Computer Aides

Beacon Corporation
1173 W. Country Creek Drive
So. Jordan, UT 84095
800-727-2427   FAX 801-254-1538
Homespun Software

Inspire Graphics
P.O. Box 935
Pleasant Grove, UT  84062
www.inspiregraphics.com
inspire@itsnet.com
800-250-3988   wholesale 801-796-9393
FAX 801-785-3878
Lettering Delights and other scrapbook computer programs

Lucie Arnaz
ETE/Konami Distributor
900 Deerfield Pkwy
Buffalo Grove, IL  60089-4510
www.lucyplace.com
800-200-7000   847-215-5100
retailers 914-232-1515
How to Save Your Family History computer program

Micro Dynamics Electronic Publishing, Inc.
703 South State St. #9
Orem, UT 84058
www.familybase.com
888-327-6472   801-431-0531
Family Base program by Timeless Software

# Miscellaneous

Les' Steel Rule Die Co.
1926 3/4 N. Doreen Ave.
So. El Monte, CA 91733
626-575-0015   FAX 626-575-3817
custom dies

Traces
7455 N. Capital Hill
Preston, ID  83263
www.name-traces.com
800-852-1951   208-852-2295
first name and surname meaning printouts

## Rubber Stamps

Many rubber stamp companies charge for their catalogs.

All Night Media, Inc.
P.O. Box 10607
San Raphael, CA 94912
800-STAMPED

Clearsnap, Inc.
Colorbox pigment inks & rubber stamps
Box 98
Anacortes, WA 98221
www.clearsnap.com
contact@clearsnap.com
800-448-4862   360-293-6634
FAX 360-293-6699

Peddler's Pack
4570 SW Watson
Beaverton, OR 97005
800-29STAMP   503-641-9555
FAX 503-626-2643
stamps and stickers

Posh Impressions
4708 Barranca Pky
Irvine, CA 92604
www.poshimpressions.com
714-651-1735   800-421-POSH (7674)
FAX 800-422-POSH

Stamp Francisco
466 8th Street #1
San Francisco, CA 94103
415-252-5975

Tsunkineko, Inc.
Redmond, WA 98052
www.tsukineko.com
sales@tsukineko.com

# Events

Sponsors of most of these events ask that you send a self-addressed, stamped envelope to receive information.

Annual Scrapbook & Rubber Stamp Convention
Creatively Yours
P.O. Box 100964
Denver, CO 80250-0964
CrYours@aol.com
303-699-4615   FAX 303-680-8928

Arizona Scrapbook Association
1719 W. Highland St.
Chandler, AZ 85224
602-963-2752 phone and FAX

Creative Getaways
Lake Arrowhead, CA
members.aol.com/cgetaways

Great American Scrapbook Convention
P.O. Box 295250
Lewisville, TX 75029-5250
scrapbkc@.gte.net
972-317-2399

Hobby Industry Association
P.O. Box 348
Elmwood Park, NJ 07407
www.hobby.org   hia@ix.netcom.com
201-794-1133   FAX 201-797-0657
serves the industry only,
not for consumers

Memories Expo, The Scrapbook Show
P.O. Box 3388
Zanesville, Ohio 43702-3388
www.creative-industires.com/memories
memories.expo@creative-industires.com/memories
740-452-4541 Offinger management
614-452-4541 FAX 740-452-2552

Midwest Scrapbook Convention
221 Jefferson St. N.
Wadenam, MN 56482
218-631-4966

Northwest Scrapbook & Rubber Stamp Convention
P.O. Box 7105
Boise, ID 83707
208-323-6033, 208-368-0996
208-323-0747

The Original Scrapbooking Cruise
TSIN National Scrapbook Day Event
The Scrapbooking Idea Network
P.O. Box 1947
Simi Valley, CA 93062
www.scrapbooking.com
805-520-0304 Jennia
cruise: 800-876-9399 Patti at Uniglobe

Scrapbook Expo
www.scrapbooking.com
888-252-EXPO

Scrapbookers Dream Day
P.O. Box 183
Hyde Park, UT 84318
gtpierson@juno.com

Un-Conventional Scrap & Stamp Convention
Auntie Amy Stamps
6500 Streeter Ave.
Riverside, CA 92504
www.autieamy.com
800-398-8835   909-689-2530

# Bibliography

Anderson, Marilyn, *Scrapbook Your Family Memories*, Addison, Texas: Sonburn, 1997.

Beller, Susan Provost, *Roots for Kids, A Genealogy Guide for Young People*, Maryland: Genealogical Publishing Company, 1997.

Biffle, Christopher, *The Castle of the Pearl*, New York: Harper & Row, 1990.

Bolles, Richard Nelson, *What Color is Your Parachute?* Berkeley, California: Ten Speed Press, 1997.

Brookes, Mona, *Drawing for Older Children and Teens, A Creative Method for Adult Beginners, Too*, Los Angeles: Jeremy P. Tarcher, Inc., 1991.

Caplan, Frank, Ed., *Growing-Up Years, Your Child's Record-Keeping Book*, New York: Anchor Press, 1978.

Cardozo, Peter, *The Whole Kids Do-It-Yourself Scrapbook*, New York: Bantam Books, 1979.

Chorzempa, Rosemary A., *My Family Tree Workbook, Genealogy for Beginners*, New York: Dover Publications, 1982.

Christensen, Marielen W., and Anthony J. Christensen, *Keeping Memories Alive*, Spanish Fork, Utah, 1981.

*Creating Keepsakes Scrapbook Magazine 1998 Idea Annual*, Orem, Utah: Porch Swing Publishing, Inc., 1997.

*Design and Layout Ideas for Scrapbook Pages*, St. Cloud, Minnesota: Creative Memories, 1995.

Eastman Kodak Company, Ed., *The Joy of Photography*, Reading, Massachusetts: Addison-Wesley Publishing Co., 1991.

Eaton, George T., *Conservation of Photographs*, Kodak Publications, 1998.

Edwards, Betty, *Drawing on the Right Side of the Brain, A Course in Enhancing Creativity and Artistic Confidence*, Los Angeles: J.P. Tarcher, Inc., 1979.

Edwards, Nancy R., *Roses in December: My Life Story and Other Memories*, Atlanta: Strawberry Patch, 1989.

Emberly, Ed, *Picture Pie 2: A Drawing Book and Stencil*, Boston: Little, Brown & Co., 1996.

Emberly, Ed, *Picture Pie: A Circle Drawing Book*, Boston: Little, Brown & Co., 1984.

Green, Donna, *To My Daughter, With Love: A Mother's Memory Book*, Cohasset, Massachusetts: Vermilion, Inc. 1993.

Greene, Bob, and D.G. Fulford, *To Our Children's Children: Preserving Family Histories for Generations to Come*, New York: Doubleday, 1993.

Gruenig, Dee, *The Great Rubber Stamp Book*, New York: Sterling Publishing Co., Inc., 1996.

Hallman, Anita Young, *Self Preservation: A Complete Guide*, Salt Lake City, Utah: Deseret Book, 1997.

Hot Off The Press, Ed. Mary Margaret Hite, Tara Choate, and Katie Hacker, *The Ultimate Book of Memory Albums*, Little Rock, Arkansas: LeisureArts, 1997.

Isidro, Tracey L., *Punch Happy, Punch Art Secrets for Scrapbooks and Gifts*, Bountiful, Utah: Living Vision Press, 1998.

Jackson, Paul, *The Pop-Up Book: Step-By-Step Instructions for Creating Over 100 Original Paper Projects*, New York: Henry Holt & Co., 1994.

Johnson, Ali, and Dianne J. Hook, *It's About Time*, Sandy, Utah: D.J. Inkers, 1996.

Julian, Stacy, and Terina Darcey, *Core Composition*, Salt Lake City, Utah: Apple of Your Eye, 1997.

Keefe, Laurence E., and Dennis Inch, *The Life of a Photograph, Archival Procesing, Matting, Framing, and Storage*. Boston: Focal Press, 2nd ed. 1990.

Miller, Ilene Chandler, *Preserving Family Keepsakes, Do's and Dont's*, Yorba Linda, California: Shumway Family History Services, 1995.

Morgan, Terri and Shmuel Thaler, *Capturing Childhood Memories: Creating an Album to Cherish, How to Photograph Your Child's Most Special Moments*, Berkeley Publications, 1996.

Ostrom, Linday, *The ABC's of Creative Lettering*, Carlstadt, New Jersey: EK Success, Ltd. 1997.

Paulsen, Deirdre M. and Jeanne S. English, *Preserving the Precious*, Salt Lake City, Utah: Restoration Source, 1988.

Reed, Brenda Lee, *Easy-to-Make Decorative Paper Snowflakes*, New York: Dover Publications, 1987.

Rempel, Siegfried, *The Care of Photographs*, 1987.

Rich, Chris, *The Book of Paper Cutting*, New York: Sterling Publishing Co., 1993.

Server, Bridgette, *Snip Your Snapshots and Trim Your Treasures*, Canby, Oregon: Hot Off The Press, 1995.

Striker, Susan. *The Fourth Anti-Coloring Book*, New York: Henry Holt & Co.,1981.

Tippetts, Nathan, *Basic Preservation and Archival Techniques*, Utah, 1994.

Tuttle, Craig A., *An Ounce of Preservation: A Guide to the Care of Papers and Photographs*, Highland City, Florida: Rainbow Books, Inc., 1995.

Wendlinger, Bob, *The Memory Triggering Book*, Oakland, California: Proust Press.

Wilhelm, Henry, and Carol Brower, *The Permanence and Care of Color Photographs: Traditional and Digital Color Prints, Color Negatives, Slides and Motion Pictures*. Grinnel, Iowa: Preservation Publishing Company, 1993.

# Glossary

## A

**Acid** - A substance that is chemically active when dissolved in water. It reacts with a base, or alkaline substance, to form a salt. These actions can weaken the cellulose in paper and cloth and make them become brittle.

**Acid migration** - The transfer, or movement, of acid from an acidic material to a less acidic or pH neutral material that touches the acidic object. This transfer can come from acidic paper, skin oils, air pollution, or any acidic substance that comes in direct contact with a more alkaline object.

**Acid-free** - A term describing materials having a pH value of 7.0 or above. Marketing alert: Only items that can be dissolved in water have a measurable pH level. You cannot give a pH for many plastics. In this case, acid-free has about as much meaning as fat-free cigarettes. It's true, but meaningless.

**Acronyms** - A series of letters in which each letter stands for a word. ABC is the acronym meaning American Broadcasting System. Unique acronyms, such a LOL for "laughing out loud" are used extensively on the Internet. A short list is included in the Cyber Support chapter.

**Acrylic** - A plastic used in making adhesives, sheets, and films. It is very stable chemically as well as weather resistant, color-fast, rigid, and transparent.

**Albumen prints** - Made from the 1850s to the 1910s, this photographic process employed egg whites, sodium chloride, and silver nitrate to make card photographs. They had a tendency to curl, so they were mounted on cardboard to protect them and keep them flat. Cartes-de-viste (2 1/4" by 4 1/4", mid 1850s to late 1860s), Cabinet cards (4 1/4" by 6 1/2", mid 1860s to 1900), Victoria cards (3 1/4" by 5", early 1870s to late 1880s), Promenade cards (4" by 7", mid 1870s to late 1890's), Imperial cards (almost 8" by 10", late 1870s to 1900), Boudoir cards (5" by 8 1/4", late 1870s to 1900), and Stereograph cards (double image giving a 3-D effect when viewed through a stereoscope, late 1850s to late 1910s) could be albumen prints. By the late 1880s, most card photographs used a dry gelatin emulsion. Yellowish highlights in the image indicate the card photograph is probably an albumen print. Albumen prints are sensitive to alkaline substances and their emulsions should not be placed in contact with buffered paper. They are also very prone to deterioration for many reasons, including the high lignin board on which most of them were mounted. You would be wise to have copies made of any albumen prints you value.

**Analogous colors** - Colors near one another on the color wheel. When combined, these colors harmonize and do not create sharp contrast.

**Archival boxes** - Well-constructed boxes made of lignin-free, acid-free paper of a high grade. For long-term storage, purchase boxes that have been tested and are sold by reputable archival suppliers. Boxes sold in stores for storing videos and photographs are frequently very low quality and acidic.

**Archival quality** - When used by a conservationist, this usually means materials that are durable, chemically inert, and proven to be very long-lasting; suitable to use in archiving or long storage of valuable records and objects. Unfortunately, most of the time you find the term today it is meaningless, because it is being used to sell products, not to describe.

**Art air gun** - A small plastic bulb attached to a pen holder that is used to blow ink off of any felt tip type pen. The effect is a soft shading of color or a splatter effect.

# B

**Balance** - A principle of design that seeks equilibrium or a harmonious integration of elements in a work of art. By manipulating the elements in the design with attention to their optical weight, balance is achieved.

**Baseball card pages** - These plastic pocket pages are designed to display collectible sports cards in a three-ring album. They have nine small pockets per page and are widely used by scrapbook enthusiasts to store stickers in three-ring binders.

**BBS or Bulletin Board System** - An electronic message board that allows viewers to read the ongoing threads, or questions and answers, posted on a specific topic. They may also participate by posting their own messages. (See the Cyber Support chapter for more information.)

**Bone folder** - A strong, smooth spatula-shaped rounded tool used to make clean creases and to smoothly secure pressure-sensitive items to a page.

**Bookmarks** - For Internet use, these are a collection of web site addresses that can be stored and then used to quickly access the web sites on your computer. (See the Cyber Support chapter for more information.)

**Brayer** - A tool with a handle and roller used to roll color onto a page. It is a rubber stamping implement that can be used with pigment ink from stamp pads or pens to decorate an album page.

**Buffering** - A substance or process used to counteract the acid in paper. Calcium carbonate and magnesium carbonate are alkaline chemicals used to buffer paper products. Buffering will help keep high quality, lignin-free paper acid-free over time. It protects the paper from acids in the environment. A buffered album page is not a magic charm that protects photographs from high acid materials like newsprint. The buffering will absorb some of the acid but may not be sufficient to prevent acid migration to the prints on the page.

# C

**CD-ROM or compact disk** - Compact disks are a very durable medium for storing digital information. For the longest-lasting record of family photo keepsakes, consider copies stored on compact disks with a plan to recopy the information in about 50 years or before, if a more durable storage technology comes available.

**Cellulose** - The main component in the cell walls of plants. This is the stable component that is less prone toward deterioration while lignin in paper is believed to be responsible for quick chemical degradation. Cotton is 100% cellulose and high alpha wood pulp can contain as much as 93% cellulose.

**Chat Room** - An interactive service provided at a web site that allows viewers to read messages as they are posted and immediately post replies. A forum for on-line discussions to take place. (See the Cyber Support chapter for more information.)

**Circle cutter** - A small device that holds paper in place while a blade attachment is used to cut a perfect circle from paper or a photo.

**Clip art** - Black and white or color art images that can be copied to use as page decorations. Colored clip art refers to images copied from a computer program or web site and printed out to use in a scrapbook. Black and white art can be copied by computer or from a book.

**Color** - The aspect of a design element that indicates the hue or specific color family such as red, green, or blue.

**Color fastness** - The ability of a colored material or ink to keep true color over time.

**Compass and swivel knife** - An X-Acto product designed to cut a perfect circle with the knife portion of the devise. However, the knife is removable and the compass can then be used with a pen to draw a perfect circle for page decoration.

**Complementary colors** - The two colors directly opposite one another on the color wheel. Red and green, blue and orange, violet and yellow make up the primary complimentary pairs.

**Conservation** - The care and treatment of artifacts, including photographs, to stabilize and maintain them. Repair and fortification processes may be included if needed. The goal of conservation is to prolong the useful life of the object to make it last as long as possible.

**Contrast** - The opposition or juxtaposition of colors, values, lines or shapes in a design that sets off and draws attention to an element or elements. Contrast is used extensively in design to create emphasis and visually interesting work.

**Coolness** - Emotional and visual quality of a color that has blue undertones such as green, blue, violet, and gray. Warm colors can have an element of coolness to them, especially slightly violet reds, pale yellows, and bluish browns.

**Copy negative** - A negative made by taking a photograph of a photographic print. This process has the preservation advantage of creating a negative from which many copies can be made economically. The main disadvantage is that the negative and the resulting copies will have a higher contrast in values than the original. Some of the subtle shading and shadows will be lost or become much darker.

**Corner edgers** - Scissors-like tools that trim paper and photo corners in a decorative shape.

**Corner rounder** - A small punch or a larger metal machine that trims the corner from a photo or paper leaving a rounded shape.

**Craft knife** - Commonly known by the brand name X-acto. Available with stable or swiveling blades. They are especially useful to cut shapes from the middle of a piece of paper, to cut slits, or make straight cuts with the help of a metal ruler.

**Crop** - 1. To cut a photo to improve its appearance. 2. A gathering of scrapbookers who crop photos and create album pages together. Those attending use the tools owned by the consultant who sponsors the workshop.

**Cutting mat** - Special plastic mat that is used for protecting the work surface when cutting with a mat knife.

**Cycling** - Changes in temperature and humidity that are particularly harmful to photographic materials. The cycling - hot during the day, much cooler at night - environment of attics is the main reason they should be avoided when storing photos.

# D

**D-ring album** - A three-ring binder album with rings made in the shape of a 'D'. This design allows the pages to lie flat against each other rather than bunching up along the inside edges.

**Deacidification** - Methods used to stop the acidic activity in a material such as paper. Rinsing is one method. Spraying the item with a buffering solution such as Wei T'o (magnesium ethyl carbonate, buffering agent) or Bookkeepers spray (magnesium oxide, buffering agent) is another method. The spray method actually deacidifies the item and buffers it as well. A more accurate description of this process would be neutralizing and buffering or alkalizing the acidic items.

**Deckle edge scissors** - A very popular paper edger that creates a look like a torn edge or the look of older snapshot edges and old fashioned photo mats.

**Deckle edge trimmer** - A small swivel blade papercutter that cuts a straight deckled edge.

**Die Cut** - A shape made from paper by cutting it out with a metal die in a die cut machine. These shapes can be cut by consumers at many scrapbook stores and at some libraries. They are also available to purchase individually and in packets.

**Digital image** - This is an image that is stored as a set of fixed values. It can then be reproduced exactly. Copies of digital images are identical to the original as long as they are made while the original storage material is undamaged. CDs are very durable and can store digital images in original condition for decades.

**Document tape** - Tape available from archival supply companies to use in repairing torn paper. It is a paper tape with a photo-safe adhesive and is sold under the names Filmoplast® P and P1 and Archival Document Repair Tape.

**Download** - To transfer software, text, or images to your computer from another computer or database via the Internet.

**DPI** - Dots per inch, a measurement that indicates the clarity of the resolution of a bitmapped image, such as those scanned and used on computers.

**Dye** - A colorant that penetrates the object being colored. Dyes are frequently unstable and prone to fading and running.

# E

**E-mail** - Electronic mail, a message sent from one person to another via the Internet.

**E-mail loop or list** - A service that connects several persons with a common interest by e-mail. When a person sends an e-mail to the appropriate address, the message goes to all who have subscribed to the list. Each subscriber also receives all the messages sent by any member to the list address. (See the Cyber Support chapter for more information.)

**Electronic scrapbook** - A collection of photos, journaling, and other scanned images that are all stored electronically. Software is available to help you construct one. (See the Cyber Support chapter for more information.)

**Embossing** - Dry embossing is the process of using a metal stencil and stylus to press a design into paper, producing a raised image. Heat embossing uses pigment ink, embossing powder, and a heat source such as an embossing gun to permanently bond a raised coating over the ink design by heat setting it.

**Embossing stencils** - Metal stencils used with an embossing stylus to impress a raised design on a piece of paper.

**Emphasis** - A principle of design that seeks to draw attention to certain elements of a design to create interest or emphasize an aspect of the design that the artist considers important. Emphasis is created through variety and contrast.

**Emulsion** - The coating on the front, or image side, of a photo.

**Encapsulation** - Enclosing a document between two sheets of stiff Mylar D® or Mellinex™ polyester plastic and partially sealing the capsule. It can be sealed with special double-sided tape such as 3M #415 . Using a nylon thread, the seal can be made by zig-zag stitching the edges of the plastic. The method provides physical support, protection from the environment, and is completely reversible by carefully trimming off one edge of the capsule to remove the document. Recommended for preserving paper documents, not photos.

# F

**Fancy rulers** - These rulers have a deckled, scalloped, wavy, or other decorative edge and are used to draw lines or borders on scrapbook pages.

**FAQs - Frequent Asked Questions** - This is a type of document frequently posted on Web sites to avoid a lot of repetition on message boards and other on-line information services. It contains questions and answers pertaining to the subject of the on-line service. It is a good idea to read this before posting on-line.

**Ferrotype** - 1. A tintype photograph 2. An undesired effect in which a photograph or negative sticks to a glossy surface such as plastic or glass due to moisture accumulation. 3. A photographic process using heat, pressure, and a polished metal sheet to create a highly glossy surface on a black and white print.

**Fiber-based prints** - These photos are printed on fiber-based paper. They can be distinguished from RC prints by checking the back of the print. Fiber-based prints feel like regular paper with no slick coating. Modern photos made before 1970 are probably printed on fiber-based paper. Extra care needs to be taken in mounting these prints since adhesives will penetrate the fiber back and be hard to remove without damaging the photo.

**Flex-Hinge Album** - Strap-bound patented album design made by the Antioch Company and sold primarily under the names Creative Memories and Webway.

**Focal point** - The element in a work that the artist chooses for the primary emphasis in a design.

**Focus** - To direct attention to an element of a design or the object of that attention.

**Fonts** - Various type styles or forms of lettering. There are computer programs that contain fonts designed especially for scrapbook use. Lettering Delights by Inspire Graphic and the D.J.Inkers collections are examples. Fonts can also be obtained by downloading them from the Internet. (See the Cyber Support chapter for more information.)

# H

**Harmony** - The overall sense that a design is visually pleasing and that the elements work together as a whole.

**Homepage** - Primary Web page of an individual or organization that contains links to access the rest of the information on the site.

# I

**Imprintables** - Stationery that has a large blank or very lightly colored space in the middle. These papers provide a space for information to be printed, such as the writing on an invitation. They are useful in albums because of the frame effect that is created by this type of design.

**Intensity** - The aspect of a design element that indicates the brightness or dullness of an object or color. A muted or grayed color has low intensity, a true color has high intensity.

**Internet** - Interconnected set of computer networks.

# J

**Jeeping** - Stiff paper edges of album pages made by the Creative Memories company. This feature adds support to the pages and acts as a spacer so pages can still lie flat after being mounted with photos.

**Journaling** - Written personal history information that stands alone or describes the people, places, events, time frame, details and emotions that go with photographs.

# L

**Lamination** - Permanently bonding clear plastic film to one or both sides of an object. Usually high heat and pressure are part of the process. All forms of lamination are nonreversible and many types use acidic adhesives.

**Laser copy** - The high quality photocopy made on special machines and frequently referred to as color copies. This process can also be used to create very high quality reproductions in black and white. Color photographs can be copied on the black and white setting to obtain inexpensive black and white prints for hand-tinting or to achieve a striking and different look.

**Layout** - The design of a scrapbook page or the two adjacent pages of a spread.

**Light box** - A box with a translucent or clear top and a light source inside that is used to illuminate paper or photographs for tracing, drawing cropping guidelines, or doing dry embossing.

**Lignin** - An organic substance closely allied to cellulose which forms the essential part of woody fibers. Lignin is present in the wood pulp used to make paper and must be removed to create a high quality, long-lasting paper. Lignin in paper is problematic because it becomes more and more acidic as it deteriorates over time. The yellow color of a newspaper left in the sun for two days is an example of the effect of lignin on paper. Many photo conservation specialists consider lignin to be very specifically harmful to photographs.

**Line** - Type of design element that defines an edge of a shape or a long narrow mark.

**Link** - A connection. On a Web page, it is a button or set of words that can connect a viewer to another page by clicking on it with the mouse.

# M

**Mat** - 1. A window cut piece of art board, mat board, or museum board used to enhance a photograph and keep it from coming in direct contact with glass or acrylic sheeting used in framing the picture. 2. In scrapbooks, a mat is usually a piece of cardstock mounted behind a photograph to enhance its appearance on a page. Overlay window cut mats are also used, usually with Polaroid prints, studio portraits, or other pictures the scrapbook compiler decides should not be cut.

**Mat knife** - Commonly known by the brand name X-acto. Available with stable or swiveling blades. They are especially useful to cut shapes from the middle of a piece of paper, to cut slits, or make straight cuts with the help of a metal ruler.

**Metal edge ruler** - Ruler made of all metal or with a metal edge that is useful to use as a guide when cutting straight lines with a mat knife.

**Module** - This is a sticker term that means all of the stickers on the strip in the area between two lines of perforations.

**Movement** - A principle of design that seeks to draw the viewer's eye to different elements of the design and create a sense of vitality and energy. Movement is achieved through arrangement of all design elements, but particularly through the use of line and repetition of elements.

**Muted colors** - Colors that have a low intensity and are slightly grayed.

# N

**Negative space** - The background space of a design.

**Neutral colors** - Colors with no definite primary or secondary color wheel hue such as grays, tans, browns, black, and white. These colors tend to take on the appearance of bright colors that are next to them in a design to blend and create harmony.

# O

**Optical weight** - A way of visually measuring elements in a design to decide how they can be used to create balance. Objects that are darker, bigger, brighter, or more detailed have greater optical weight.

# P

**Page protector** - A plastic envelope that contains a scrapbook page or slips over it. See "sheet protector."

**P.A.T. or Photographic Activity Test** - A test developed by the American National Standards Institute to determine what chemical interactions occur between photographs and enclosures, or other materials, used in proximity to photos while in storage. Accelerated aging tests using high heat and humidity levels mimic the natural aging process. This provides information that allows scientists to approximate what will happen to the photographs stored with these materials over time. If a product passes the P.A.T., it is highly unlikely to accelerate the rate at which a photo would normally deteriorate.

**Paper crimper** - Paper is threaded through this device to crimp it uniformly. The result is a corrugated shape.

**Papercutter** - A large tool used to cut straight edges on paper while keeping the corners squared and the cuts perpendicular. In addition to the common swivel blade variety, cutters are also available with round rolling blades. The second type presents less danger to small children and some brands offer several blades that can cut the paper leaving a decorative edge.

**Paper edgers** - Special scissors that trim a decorative edge on paper. Also called decorative scissors or fancy scissors.

**Paper trimmer** - A small version of a paper cutter that may have a knife arm blade or a tiny sliding blade.

**Password** - Secret code that allows some privacy in on-line communication. A password usually must be entered in order to open an e-mail box.

**Pattern paper** - Paper with an overall repeated design such as gingham or hearts.

**Pen-stitch** - A decoration technique in which small lines are drawn on or around objects to mimic the look of stitches.

**Perspective** - A principle of design that creates a sense of depth or the technique of depicting three-dimensionality and spatial relationships on a flat surface. It is created through overlapping elements, placement of elements on a page, use of color and value, and by converging lines.

**pH** (potential of hydrogen) - A measurement of the alkalinity or acidity of an object that is water soluble.

**pH neutral** - The pH of water; in the middle of the scale - not acid or alkaline.

**pH scale** - The range of acidity or alkalinity indicated by the numbers 0-14. A pH of 0 or 1 is very highly acidic and pH of 14 is very highly alkaline. Paper with a pH of 5 is ten times as alkaline as paper with a pH of 6. Paper with a pH of 5 is considered to be highly acidic and buffered paper typically has a pH of between 7 and 9.

**pH test pen** - A pen that applies a pH indicator chemical to paper. The chemical changes color to indicate acidity or alkalinity.

**Photo and slide cleaner** - Solution formulated to clean oils, adhesives, and other residues from photographs and slides. PEC-12® is an excellent cleaner.

**Photo corners** - Tiny self-adhesive triangular holders that fit onto the corners of a photo and allow it to be mounted onto a page. With this method, no adhesive touches the photo. They are available in clear plastic, paper, and laser cut paper.

**Photo oils** - Oil paints formulated especially to use in hand tinting black and white photographs.

**Photo-safe** - In this book, the term is used to mean objects, materials, and processes that will in no way shorten the life or damage the condition of photographs. Any product that has passed the P.A.T. is considered photo-safe by this definition. Other products, such as well-made acid-free, lignin-free colorfast paper are considered to be photo-safe, because so much research has been done on almost identical materials. It is not a legal term. A product labeled photo-safe must provide test results or an ingredient list to support the claim before you assume the product will not damage photographs.

**Pigment** - Colorants that are used to create a stable, permanent ink. Pigment-based inks sit on the surface of paper and remain chemically inert. Many of these inks are highly fade resistant, waterproof, and colorfast. Poor quality pigments exist. Even pigment inks need to be tested before being judged appropriate for archival purposes.

**Plasticizer** - Chemical additive that increases flexibility and elasticity and is usually detrimental to photographs and should be avoided in album products.

**Polyester** - For archival purposes, this refers to a specific type of polyester sold under the names Mylar D® and Mellinex™ #516, the common name for the plastic polyethylene terephthalate. It is one of the most inert and stable plastics developed and is transparent, strong and stiff, but has a tendency to create static cling.

**Polyethylene** - An inert plastic that is considered by most conservators to be safe for photographic archival use. Some professionals consider only some polyethylene products to be safe. It is flexible and translucent.

**Polypropylene** - A stable plastic generally regarded as excellent for use around photos as long as it is not coated. This plastic must be coated to accept an imprint such as a manufacturer's name. For use with photos, the side touching the photos should not be coated. It should be untreated, virgin plastic. It is clear and somewhat stiff.

**Positive space** - The elements of a design placed on a page.

**Posting** - To place a message on a message board, e-mail loop, or other on-line communication service.

**Precision cutting knife** - Another name for the mat knife sold under the brand name X-Acto.

**Preservation** - A broad term meaning to maintain valuable records and artifacts in as close as possible to their original condition. This task may include making copies of items when it is impossible or not practical to stop the deterioration process in the original.

**Print-to-print process** - A photographic reproduction process allowing the creation of a copy directly from the original print with no use of a negative. Color laser copies, as well as copies made on photographic paper by processes created by Kodak and Fuji are example of this process.

**Punches** - Metal and plastic craft tools used to punch shapes from paper. It also sometimes refers to the shape that has been punched out. Corner punches are used on the corner of a piece of paper, a page, or a photo. They cut a design out at the corner edges and sometimes also round the corner. Hand-held punches are a variation of the small hole punchers used to punch paper to fit in a three-ring binder. They punch out a tiny shape such as a heart, a star, a teardrop, or several sizes of circles.

**PVA or Polyvinyl acetate** - A clear, solid plastic used in adhesives. If it is internally plasticized, it is chemically stable and reversible with application of water and thus suitable for archival purposes.

**PVC or Polyvinyl Chloride** - This very chemically active plastic emits a chloride gas which combines with moisture in the air to create hydrochloric acid. This chemical is very destructive. An example is its tendency to lift the print from a photocopy that is left in contact with a vinyl notebook.

# Q

**Quilter's 1/4-inch disc** - A small metal disc used with a pencil to trace an outline exactly 1/4" out from the edge of an object. This works best for tracing around objects at least as thick as cardstock and with generally smooth contours and no sharp in-cut corners.

# R

**Red-eye pen** - A pen with a very fine point that deposits a bit of green ink on the red eye portion of a photo.

**Resin-coated or RC prints** - Almost all snapshots today are printed on resin-coated paper. They are easy to identify because the back of the print is slick and shiny due to the resin. Most prints made since the early 1970s are RC prints.

**Reversible** - A procedure or action done to an artifact, such as a photo, that can be undone with no damage occurring to the object. This is a basic requirement of sound preservation techniques. If a photo is mounted in such a way that it cannot be removed without being damaged, the mounting is nonreversible.

# S

**Scanner** - A machine that "reads" a visual image, like a photograph, and changes it into digital information that can be stored electronically. These images can be manipulated and changed with software programs, printed out on a printer, and sent to others via e-mail. (See the Cyber Support chapter for more information.)

**Scherenschnitte** - The German art of cutting elaborate and beautiful designs from paper using fine tipped scissors or a cutting knife.

**Seam roller** - A small roller with a handle used to press seams flat and useful in applying pressure to items to make them adhere strongly to an album page when mounted with adhesive or pressure sensitive tape.

**Self-stick "magnetic" album** - Albums with adhesive-coated pages which are then covered with a sheet of clear plastic that adheres to the page on any areas that have no photos on them. These albums are known for having the photos stick to the page and being impossible to remove. Many have acidic or chemically active adhesives and plastics that damage the emulsion of photos. Even modern self-stick albums with higher quality plastics and adhesives are not recommended, because they may still present problems with photos sticking stubbornly when there is a need to remove them.

**Service provider** - An organization that provides access to the Internet including large companies such as America Online, local companies, and universities.

**Shade** - A true color hue with black added, or a dark color.

**Shape** - A type of design element that contains space with a line that is continuous. A distinct form with definite height and width.

**Sheet protectors** - Clear plastic envelopes that are used to protect memory album pages when they are viewed and stored. Sheet protectors for three-ring binder albums allow a standard 8 1/2" by 11" sheet of card stock or paper to be used as an album page. The page slips in the top or the inside edge of the protector. Albums with this type of protector are also available in a 12" x 12" size as well. Other styles of sheet protectors wrap around the album page or slip on from the side.

**Silica gel canister** - A preservation supply that is used to absorb moisture from the air and reduce the relative humidity in a contained space. Also called desiccants, silica gel granules can be heated to make them release the moisture they have absorbed and can then be reused. Granules are available that signal when they reach a saturation point, and need to be dried out, by changing color.

**Slipcase** - A hard-sided case that comes with an album and is used to protect it and provide extra structural support during storage or transportation.

**Slipcover** - A cloth cover used to slip over an album and provide dust protection while the album is being stored.

**Space** - The parts of the page that remain empty.

**Spam** - Electronic junk mail, usually advertising but occasionally a chain letter, propaganda, or other information, that comes through user groups or individual e-mails.

**Spot pens** - Pens used to hand tint black and white photographs. For most people they are much easier to use than photo oil paints.

**Spread** - The two scrapbook pages that are next to each other when the book is opened. If these pages are considered together when they are designed, the result is more visually appealing. Even if a viewer is looking at one page, both are seen when the album is open.

**Stabilio pencil** - A brand name soft pencil that can be used to mark on the back of photos or to trace shapes for cropping on the front of a photo. The markings can be wiped off the photo front with a soft cloth. These pencils are available in blue and white.

**Stationery** - Usually paper designed to use for letter writing, but adopted for use on album pages. The design may be a border or it may cover the page. This paper comes in several sizes and thicknesses.

**Stencils** - These are plastic sheets with various designs cut out. They are used with paints, inks, colored pencils, and pens to trace or stencil the design on a page or paper. See also embossing stencils.

**Stylus** - A metal tool with a small smooth ball tip that is used in dry embossing and to score fold lines in paper.

**Swap** - A friendly exchange of scrapbook supplies organized through Web sites, e-mail loops, and e-mail messages. Birthday swaps, secret pal swaps, and sticker swaps are different varieties that exist. (See the Cyber Support chapter for more information.)

**Symmetry** - Balance achieved by placing identical elements on two sides of a design, also known as formal balance.

**T**

**Tape runner** - A small dispenser that holds a roll of double-sided tape that is cut into small pieces. By pressing the holder against a page and pulling gently, the bits of tape are stuck down on photos or paper. The item can then be mounted on a scrapbook page. The tape runner can place one or two tiny pieces of tape on an object or many pieces that act as a large strip of tape.

**Templates** - Plastic sheets with cut-out shapes of varying sizes. The shapes available are ovals, circles, other geometrics, stars, hearts, and a wide variety of holiday and nature objects. They are used to trace the shape onto a photo and cut the photo into that shape. They may also be used to trace and cut shapes from paper to use as mats for photographs and page decorations.

**Texture** - A type of design element that creates the visual and tactile quality of the surface of the work.

**Thread** - A series of questions and answers on one topic, or an on-line discussion, that is posted on a message board or BBS.

**Time capsule** - A container for keepsakes designed to contain objects that tell the story of the time the capsule is assembled and sealed. Kits are sold which include the capsule, instructions, and even items to fill in and include to commemorate a special event such as a birth, wedding, or graduation. Most affordable capsules are not intended for burying. They are sealed, stored in a cool dry place and then opened many years later.

**Tint** - A true color hue with white added, or a light color.

**Tintypes** - Collodion process photographs that are direct, positive images with bases of lacquered metal. They were made between 1856 and the late 1890s but were not popular after the mid 1870s. They have dull, grayish images and black or brown metal bases. If you have tintypes or any nonpaper photographs, have a high quality copy made and consult an informed conservation supplier about what materials to use in storing the original photographs in archival wrappings and boxes.

# U

**Unity** - A principle of design that seeks to create harmony between the elements of an artwork in order to produce a single primary effect or message. Unity is created through balance and repetition of elements.

# V

**Value** - An aspect of a design element that indicates the degree of lightness or darkness.

**Vinyl** - A wide variety of plastics, many of which are very chemically active and may damage photographs. PVC that is used to cover common school and business binders is a very aggressive type of vinyl that should definitely not be used around photos. Photo-safe plastics include certain polyesters, some polyethylene, polypropylene, polyvinyl acetate, and acrylic.

**Virus** - Software that infects other software and causes damage to a computer system and the information it contains. It is important to have a virus protection program if you are going to download information from the Internet and to be cautious about what you download.

# W

**Warmth** - Emotional and visual quality of a color that has yellow or red undertones such as yellow, orange, most reds, and brown. Cool colors can have an element of warmth to them, especially yellow-greens, muted violets, and yellow-grays.

**Web site** - A location accessed on the Internet that contains various types of information and information services. On scrapbooking web sites, pictures of layouts, product information, articles, event announcements, message boards (BBS), chat rooms, store listings, and many more features can be found. (See the Cyber Support chapter for more information.)

**White space** - Another term for negative space or the background of a design. The term is used to emphasize the need to look at this space as a design element in and of itself.

**World Wide Web or WWW** - Hypermedia system that provides access to information through clients such as Netscape and Mosaic.

**Workshop** - In scrapbooking, this usually means a gathering of scrapbookers who crop photos and create album pages together. Those attending use the tools owned by the consultant or store that sponsors the workshop.

# *Index*

**Living Vision Press**
P.O. Box 326
Bountiful, Utah 84011
www.inconnect.com/~lvision
801-292-6007

You may order the following titles directly from the publisher:

## A Lasting Legacy
### Scrapbooks and Photo Albums that Touch the Heart                    $19.95
by Souzzann Y.H. Carroll

As our lives become busier, the important things become more important. Our families, friends, and treasured experiences are sources of joy that we want to revisit again and again. *A Lasting Legacy* is a guide to creating memory albums that are meaningful, attractive, and made to last and be enjoyed. The book includes many practical resources, including a list of Top Tips at the end of each chapter, to summarize the information and make it easy to find. Over 180 sources of retail and wholesale supplies are included in the resource appendix. The book is 168 pages, 8 in color, and has many illustrations.

## Punch Happy
### Punch Art Secrets for Scrapbooks and Gifts
by Tracey L. Isidro with Souzzann Y.H. Carroll                    $14.95
(available spring 1998)
64 pages, including 16 in color

This comprehensive guide to using widely available craft paper punches describes very simple ways to create beautiful and complex designs. Animals, flowers, and borders are among the hundreds of ideas which include simple, detailed instructions and complete illustrations. Completed project patterns include scrapbook pages, greeting cards, and gifts.

This one-of-a-kind book will show you how to turn all your scraps of paper into clever, fun designs to be used for memory albums, cards and many other creative craft projects. Because the punch art ideas can be done from left over bits of paper, this is a very economical approach to page decoration. Many of the creations require use of just a few basic, versatile punches. Step-by-step guidance in creating the designs and many illustrations make this book a "must-have" for your collection.
View Tracey's designs on-line now at the Scrap Happy Website:
www.telepath.com/bcarson/scrap_happy/punch.html

To order, send the cost of the book, $2.00 shipping and handling per book, and sales tax if you are a Utah resident. Please write or call for wholesale prices and shipping costs on orders of more than 4.